NUT**SHELLS**

Family Law

NINTH EDITION

by
TONY WRAGG
University Principal Tutor, Law,
University of Derby

SWEET & MAXWELL

THOMSON REUTERS

First Edition – 1989
Second Edition – 1992
Third Edition – 1995
Fourth Edition – 1998
Fifth Edition – 2001
Sixth Edition – 2004
Seventh Edition – 2007
Eighth Edition – 2010

Published in 2013 by Sweet & Maxwell
part of Thomson Reuters (Professional) UK Limited
(Registered in England and Wales, Company No. 1679046. Registered Office and address
for service: Aldgate House, 33 Aldgate High Street, London EC3N 1DL)

For further information on our products and services, visit
www.sweetandmaxwell.co.uk

Typeset by YHT Ltd., London
Printed by Ashford Colour Press, Gosport, Hants

No natural forests were destroyed to make this product;
only farmed timber was used and re-planted

A CIP catalogue record for this book is available from the British Library.

ISBN: 978-0-414-02571-4

Thomson Reuters and the Thomson Reuters logo are trademarks of Thomson Reuters.
Sweet & Maxwell ® is a registered trademark of Thomson Reuters (Professional) UK
Limited.

Crown copyright material is reproduced with the permission of the Controller
of HMSO and the Queen's Printer for Scotland.

˙˙˙˙SHELLS

Family Law

YOU'VE GOT IT
CRACKED

Nutcases – your essential revision and starter guides

- Provides you with in-depth case analysis of the facts, principles and decision of the most important cases in an area of law

- Incorporates colour to help distinguish cases and legislation and aid ease of use

- Presents the text in bite-size chunks and includes bullets where appropriate to aid navigation, assimilation and retention of information

- Breaks the subject down into key topics to enable you to easily identify and concentrate on particular topics

- Opens each chapter with a short introduction to outline the key concepts covered and condense complex and important information

- Highlights Court of Appeal and House of Lords cases to enable you to easily identify the relative significance of the cases examined

- Includes boxed "think points" at the end of each chapter providing further case analysis

- Fully indexed by individual cases and topics

Available from all good booksellers

Contents

Using this Book

DETAILED TABLE OF CONTENTS
for easy navigation.

TABLES OF CASES
AND LEGISLATION for easy reference.

CHAPTER INTRODUCTIONS
to outline the key concepts covered
and condense complex and important
information.

An Introductɩ

....
INTRODUCTION

This book considers the doctrines
by the branch of law known as "e
the concept of the trust. In part
duction to equity and trusts
development of Fɾ

**DEFINITION CHECKPOINTS,
EXPLANATION OF KEY CASES**
to highlight important information.

As mentioned, there aɾᵉ
half secret trust. It is cruciaᵢ
situations, different rules appᵢᵧ
has been created, it is necessary

A Fully Secret Trust

DEFINITION CHECKPOINT

A fully secret trust operates in ciɾ
face of the will that the legatee ᵗ
No indication of a trust or its teᵣ
itself.

KEY CASE

are the other provisioₙ
contract of employment.

KEY CASE

CARMICHAEL V NATIONAL POWER PLC [1
Mrs Carmichael worked as a guide for
required" basis, showing groups of vi
tion. She worked some hours most wᵉ
wore a company uniform, was someᵢ
vehicle, and enjoyed many of the bᵉ
question for the court to determiₙ
"umbrella" or "global" emploᵧ
ᵗᵗʰ she worked and tʰ

DIAGRAMS, FLOWCHARTS AND OTHER DIAGRAMMATIC REPRESENTATION to clarify and condense complex and important information and breakup the text.

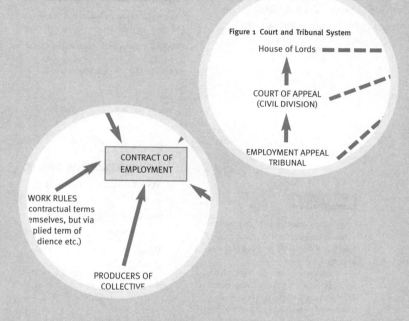

Figure 1 Court and Tribunal System

House of Lords

COURT OF APPEAL
(CIVIL DIVISION)

EMPLOYMENT APPEAL
TRIBUNAL

CONTRACT OF
EMPLOYMENT

WORK RULES
contractual terms
emselves, but via
plied term of
dience etc.)

PRODUCERS OF
COLLECTIVE

…me tra…
…ue a successful claim un…

Revision Checklist

You should now know and understand:

• the relevant provisions of the Ins

• the differences between a trar preference;

• the special bankruptcy provis¹

• the family provisions.

END OF CHAPTER REVISION CHECKLISTS outlining what you should know and understand.

END OF CHAPTER QUESTION AND ANSWER SECTION with advice on relating knowledge to examination performance, how to approach the question, how to structure the answer, the pitfalls (and how to avoid them!) and how to get the best marks.

QUESTION AND ANSWER

The Question

David and Emily are employed as machin worked for them for one and a half years

Emily discovers that David earns £9.00 paid £8.50 per hour. She also disco employed by a subsidiary of XCo in

HANDY HINTS AND USEFUL WEBSITES – revision and examination tips and advice relating to the subject features at the end of the book, along with a list of Useful Websites.

HANDY HINTS

Examination questions in employmen either essay questions or problem ques format and in what is required of the ex of question in turn.

Students usually prefer one type normally opting for the problem quest examinations are usually set in a wa least one of each style of question

Very few, if any, questions s about a topic, and it

COLOUR CODING throughout to help distinguish cases and legislation from the narrative. At the first mention, cases are highlighted in colour and italicised and legislation is highlighted in colour and emboldened.

an ethnic group (
psies are an ethnic group (CR
Rastafarians are not an ethnic grou,
ment [1993] I.R.L.R. 284)
(d) Jehovah's Witnesses are not an ethnic
Norwich City College case 1502237/97)
(e) RRA covers the Welsh (Gwynedd CC v Jon
(f) Both the Scots and the English are covere
"national origins" but not by "ethnic or
Board v Power [1997], Boyce v British Air

It should be noted that Sikhs, Jews, Jeh
arians are also protected on th
ent Equality (Religion or Be

Table of Cases

Table of Statutes

xix

DECREES RELATING TO MARRIAGE

INTRODUCTION

This Chapter is concerned with the ways that marriage and civil partnerships can be brought to an end.

1. By divorce;
2. Under the Civil Partnership Act 2004 (**CPA**);
3. By a decree of Nullity.

We will examine the respective grounds in more detail. It is perhaps worth noting at the start, that despite our high divorce rates (approximately 130,000 per year) the majority of marriages are ended by the death of one of the spouses.

DIVORCE

The ground for divorce and the five facts

Under the Matrimonial Causes Act 1973 (**M.C.A.**) there is only one ground for divorce: the petitioner must establish that the marriage has irretrievably broken down (s.1(1) of the **M.C.A.**). However, the court cannot grant a divorce unless the petitioner also proves one of five facts, as referred to in s.1(2) of the **M.C.A.**

The five facts are:

(a) that the respondent has committed adultery and the petitioner finds it intolerable to live with him;

(b) that the respondent has behaved in such a way that the petitioner cannot reasonably be expected to live with him;

(c) that the respondent has deserted the petitioner for a period of at least two years immediately preceding the presentation of the petition;

(d) that the parties have lived apart for a continuous period of at least two years immediately preceding the presentation of the petition and the respondent consents to a decree being granted; and

(e) that the parties have lived apart for a period of at least five years immediately preceding the presentation of the petition.

Figure 1: The grounds for divorce

> The respondent has committed adultery and the petitioner finds it intolerable to live with him or her.

> The respondent has behaved in such a way that the petitioner cannot reasonably be expected to live with him or her.

> The respondent has deserted the petitioner for a period of at least two years immediately preceding the presentation of the petition.

> The parties have lived apart for a continuous period of two years immediately preceding the presentation of the petition and the respondent consents to the divorce being granted.

> The parties have lived apart for a period of at least five years immediately preceding the presentation of the petition.

It must be emphasised that even if the court reaches the conclusion that the marriage has irretrievably broken down, a decree cannot be granted unless the petitioner also proves one of the five facts (see, for example, *Chilton v Chilton* (CA 1990)).

However, proof of one of the five facts does not conclusively establish irretrievable breakdown: the court can still refuse a decree if it is satisfied that the marriage has not irretrievably broken down (s.1(4) of the **M.C.A.**). Consideration will now be given to each of the five facts in turn.

Adultery (Section 1(2)(a))

This fact has two limbs. It is established that the second limb—the petitioner's finding it intolerable to live with the respondent—does not have to be caused by the first limb—the respondent's adultery (*Cleary v Cleary* (CA 1974)). This decision was reluctantly given and provoked criticism not least because of the odd results it could produce.

Adultery has been defined as "willing sexual intercourse between a married person and one of the opposite sex" (*S v S* (HC 1962)).

"Sexual intercourse" means penetration of the female by the male, however briefly (*Dennis v Dennis* (CA 1955)).

"Willing" connotes, first, that the person against whom the allegation is made should have consented to the intercourse. Thus, a woman who is raped does not thereby commit adultery.

Secondly, "willing" connotes that person has the necessary capacity to form the intent to commit adultery.

> **S. v S. (1962)**
> The husband had committed adultery with a lady insane within the definition of the McNaghten rules. She was held not to have committed adultery and dismissed from the suit.

However, if the alleged adulterer lacked capacity as a result of voluntarily consuming excess alcohol, adultery can still be found against him. The court will examine the surrounding circumstances, including the motive for drinking, in determining whether or not that party was guilty of adultery (*Goshawk v Goshawk* (HC 1965)).

In *Cleary v Cleary & Hutton* (1975) it was held that intolerability need not be by reason of the adultery: "blowing his nose too much would do".

Section 2(1) of the **M.C.A.** provides that there can be no decree if the parties have lived with each other for more than six months after the discovery of the alleged adultery.

Behaviour (Section 1(2)(b))

One of the best formulations of the principles to be applied in deciding whether or not this fact is proved is to be found in *Livingstone-Stallard v Livingstone-Stallard* (HC 1974).

> **KEY CASE**
>
> **LIVINGSTONE-STALLARD V LIVINGSTONE-STALLARD (HC 1974)**
> "Would any right thinking person come to the conclusion that this husband has behaved in such a way that this wife cannot reasonably be expected to live with him, taking into account the whole of the circumstances and the characters and personalities of the parties?"

The principle applies equally where it is the husband who is the petitioner.

There is an objective element in this test but it should also be noted that the test takes into account the characters and personalities of the actual parties concerned. This will mean, for example, that if a particular petitioner is a weak or timid character then it is unlikely that the court would not expect him to endure a level of conduct that it may expect a stronger or more forceful petitioner to withstand. Similarly, the petitioner's own conduct may be relevant as where, for example, the respondent's behaviour has been provoked.

As each case stands or falls on its own facts, it is of little use to cite numerous authorities detailing the type of behaviour that has been held to be sufficient under this fact. Such matters as violence, obsessive gambling, excessive drinking and conducting amorous, even if not adulterous, relationships with others, will usually amount to behaviour that the petitioner cannot reasonably be expected to put up with and this is perhaps not surprising.

However, conduct that on the face of it is more trivial than that already mentioned, can also amount to such behaviour if, for example, the petitioner is able to show that the conduct complained of has occurred consistently over an appreciable period of time. In this category would be such matters as threats, addressing the petitioner with abuse and/or obscene language, criticism or humiliation.

The courts have identified two types of behaviour, positive and negative or, to put it another way, acts and omissions.

It is not necessary for the respondent to have intended to harm or distress the petitioner with his behaviour or even to have intended to behave in a particular way at all.

THURLOW V THURLOW (1976)

The wife was an epileptic and suffering from a neurological disorder. As a result, over a period of a few years, her physical condition deteriorated until she became bedridden, doubly incontinent and needed assistance in feeding. During her illness, she had also caused worry by setting fire to articles of clothing and furniture, wandering in the streets at night and throwing small household items at her mother-in-law. The husband, who had made valiant efforts to cope with looking after her, was granted a decree.

CARTER-FEA V CARTER-FEA (1987)

He was unable to manage his affairs. The wife found it impossible to live in "a world of fantasy, with unpaid bills, bailiffs at the door and second mortgages". But the behaviour must be more than "just a state of affairs".

PHEASANT V PHEASANT (1972)

Husband complained that wife did not give him the "spontaneous, demonstrative affection which he craved". The petition failed: they had simply become incompatible.

Petitions based on this ground remain a striking example of the failure of the legislation to eliminate bitterness and humiliation from divorce. For example:

LIVINGSTONE-STALLARD V LIVINGSTONE-STALLARD (1974)
The husband made a long list of trivial complaints, including disputes about washing underwear and "drinking with trades people".

MASON V MASON (1980)
How often should couples have sex?

RICHARDS V RICHARDS (1974)
Amongst the wife's catalogue of complaints was the fact that he forgot her birthday and didn't buy her flowers at the birth of the child.

With regard to the provisions for living together, s.2 does not contain an absolute prohibition relating to petitions under s.1(2)(b) of the **M.C.A.** If the parties have lived with each other after the date of the last incident of behaviour alleged in the petition, then this fact is to be disregarded if they have not done so for more than six months. By implication, therefore, the court can take into account the fact that the parties have lived with each other for a period exceeding six months after the date of the last incident of behaviour alleged, when assessing whether or not the fact for divorce has been established. Thus, s.2 creates a discretionary bar to divorce for petitions under s.1(2)(b) of the **M.C.A.**

Desertion (Section 1(2)(c))

Approximately 1 per cent of divorce petitions presented rely on this ground. The concept will only briefly be discussed.

There are four conditions to be fulfilled:

(a) the parties must be physically living apart. This has the same meaning as in s.2(1)(d); [see later]
(b) the deserting spouse must have the intention to live apart permanently;
(c) the parties must not have consented to the separation; and
(d) there must be lack of good cause for leaving.

Figure 2: Conditions for desertion

Parties must be physically apart.
Deserter must have intention.
Parties must not have not consented.
Lack of good cause for leaving.

The desertion must have lasted for a continuous period of two years immediately preceding the presentation of the petition.

However, it should be noted that s.2(5) provides the "continuous nature of the separation is not to be affected by the parties having lived with each other for a period of less than six months, though no account shall be taken of that period in calculating the length of separation". For example, H left in January 2006 and returned in January 2007 for three months, then left again. Petition could not be presented until April 2008 (two years desertion plus three months of cohabitation).

Living apart (Section 1(2)(d))

The fact has two limbs: a period of living apart and the respondent's consent.

It is usually quite easy to determine that the parties are "living apart" in the physical sense. Most often, one spouse will move out of the home and go and live elsewhere. However, by s.2(6) of the **M.C.A.**, the parties are to be treated as living apart "unless they are living with each other in the same household". This provision, therefore, makes it possible for the parties to obtain a divorce under s.1(2)(d) even though they are living under the same roof, if they are living in such a way that they can be said to have established separate households. Generally this means that any sign of a communal or joint life must be absent.

> **LE BROCQ V LE BROCQ (1964)**
> Wife excluded husband from her bedroom by means of a bolt on the door: they spoke to each other only when necessary. But she cooked his meals and he paid her weekly housekeeping. Per Harman L.J.:
>
> "There was a separation of bedrooms, separation of hearts—but one household was carried on."

MOUNCER v MOUNCER (HC 1972)

The parties had separate bedrooms and the wife did not do the husband's washing. Nevertheless, the wife cooked for the family and the parties took their meals together. Both were responsible for the cleaning. The husband had refused to move out because he wanted to see and care for the children.

Held: the parties were still living with each other in the same household.

The lack of a communal life is not always the key however.

FULLER v FULLER (CA 1973)

Four years after the wife left the husband to go and live with another man, the husband became ill and was not well enough to live by himself. He moved in with the wife and her boyfriend, as a lodger, so that the wife could nurse him. The parties had separate bedrooms—indeed the wife slept with her boyfriend—but the wife cooked and washed for the husband.

Held: the parties were not living with each other in the same household because this phrase meant living with each other as husband and wife.

The concept of living apart does not only entail the physical separation of the parties. As was stated in *Santos v Santos* (CA 1972):

> "It is necessary to prove something more than that the husband and the wife are physically separated ... the relevant state of affairs does not exist whilst both parties recognise the marriage as still subsisting."

However, it is sufficient that one of the parties recognised that the marriage was at an end (even if this is the petitioner) and it is not necessary for that party to communicate the recognition to the other.

Therefore, if the parties separate because, for example, one of them is committed to prison or goes to work abroad and, at the time, both feel that the marriage is still alive, s.1(2)(d) cannot be used for divorce or at least, not until one of the parties has changed his mind about the state of the marriage and has then waited two years.

For the court to find that the marriage has irretrievably broken down on the basis that the parties have lived apart, they must have done so for at least two years immediately preceding the presentation of the petition.

Subject to s.2 of the **M.C.A.** this means that both elements of the concept of living apart must exist for two years, without a break, right up to the date of issuing the divorce petition.

Under s.1(2)(d) of the **M.C.A.**, the respondent's consent to the decree is necessary. He must therefore have the mental capacity to give that consent. This involves the respondent not only knowing what he is doing in giving consent but also understanding the consequences (*Mason v Mason* (HC 1972)).

Living apart for 5 years (Section 1(2)(e))

Under this subsection, the time period is five years immediately preceding the petition and the consent of the respondent is not required. Otherwise, the two facts are identical in law.

The definition of "living apart", applies to s.1(2)(e) also; while the facts of *Santos v Santos* involved a petition under s.1(2)(d), it was made quite clear that the necessity for at least one of the parties to have felt that the marriage was dead before they could be said to be "living apart" was equally applicable to petitions under s.1(2)(e).

Although facts (d) and (e) are so similar in law it is to be remembered that their use in practice is very different. Parties will use s.1(2)(d) when they agree that there should be a divorce, and the subsequent proceedings are often completely amicable. Petitions under s.1(2)(e) are often filed when one party is totally against the idea: as a result, the proceedings are often acrimonious.

LEGISLATION HIGHLIGHTER

Section 5 of the M.C.A. creates a defence to divorce available only to respondents to petitions based on five years separation. The respondent must establish that the dissolution of the marriage would result in "grave financial or other hardship to him and that it would in all the circumstances be wrong to dissolve the marriage."

If the court finds that the petitioner can establish another fact for divorce, as well as that under s.1(2)(e) of the **M.C.A.**, then the defence under s.5 is not available. It must be emphasised that the hardship must result from the dissolution of the marriage and not the separation of the parties. There were a number of cases, some successful, contending that loss of pension rights was grave financial hardship but the reforms relating to pension splitting and earmarking (see Ch.3) means such cases will become rare. However, in *Marchant v Marchant* (1999) the court stayed the decree until determination of ancillary relief proceedings but there was real danger that H might die, denying the wife's rights to his nearly due pension.

> **O v O (1999)**
> Husband refused to grant wife a Get, a Jewish divorce, without which she could not remarry. Decree refused on grounds of grave injustice to grant him a decree whilst he was denying her.

The Divorce (Religious Marriages) Act 2002, which came into force in February 2003, amends the **M.C.A.** and allows the court to require the dissolution of a religious marriage before granting a decree absolute.

Any respondent is entitled to defend a divorce petition on the basis that the fact for divorce alleged does not exist, but these cases are rare.

It should be noted that if the respondent is successful in defending the divorce petition, in whatever way, the marriage will not be terminated. This situation must be distinguished from a respondent who succeeds, not only in defending a divorce petition, but also in cross petitioning himself: that is in successfully establishing a fact for divorce against the petitioner. The result will then be that the marriage is terminated but that it is the respondent who has obtained the decree.

Delays A delay in the divorce process can occur for many reasons: inertia or a lack of co-operation on the part of one of the parties or the petitioner's solicitor having too great a work load. However, delay can also occur as a result of the operation of ss.10 and 41 of the **M.C.A.**, both of which are designed to ensure that the interests of persons other than the petitioner enjoy a certain measure of protection in the divorce process. A divorce is granted in two stages: decree nisi and then, usually just a few weeks later, decree absolute. Both ss.10 and 41 of the **M.C.A.** can operate to delay the grant of a decree absolute of divorce, even though the nisi has been granted on proof of irretrievable breakdown.

Section 10 of the **M.C.A.** enables the respondent to a divorce based upon either two or five years' separation to apply to the court, after the grant of a decree nisi but before the grant of a decree absolute, for his financial position to be considered. Basically, no grant of a decree absolute is then possible until the court is satisfied with the arrangements made for the respondent. This can result in a long delay.

Section 41 of the **M.C.A.**, as amended by the Children Act 1989 (**C.A.**), was designed to protect children. Note, however, that under the draft legislation issued by the Government on September 5, 2012 ("the draft Bill 2012") all issues relating to children should be referred to mediation and failing that will be the subject of **C.A.** proceedings.

CIVIL PARTNERSHIP ACT 2004

The purpose of the **C.P.A.** is to enable same-sex couples to obtain legal recognition of their relationship by forming a civil partnership. They may do so by registering as civil partners of each other provided:

(a) they are of the same sex;
(b) they are not already in a civil partnership or lawfully married;
(c) they are not within the prohibited degrees of relationship; and
(d) they are both aged 16 or over (and, if either of them is under 18 and the registration is to take place in England and Wales or Northern Ireland, the consent of the appropriate people or bodies has been obtained).

The Act also sets out the legal consequences of forming a civil partnership, including the rights and responsibilities and termination provisions.

Dissolution of civil partnership which has broken down irretrievably

Section 44(1) **C.P.A.** sets out the sole ground on which an application for dissolution may be made, namely that the civil partnership has broken down irretrievably.

In order to demonstrate the irretrievable breakdown of the civil partnership the applicant must satisfy the court of one or more of the following facts set out in ss.(5):

(a) That his or her civil partner (called the respondent for the purposes of the proceedings) has behaved in such a way that the applicant cannot reasonably be expected to live with the respondent.
(b) That the applicant and the respondent have lived apart for a continuous period of at least two years immediately preceding the application (this is referred to in the Act as "2 years' separation") and that the respondent consents to a dissolution order being made.
(c) That the applicant and the respondent have lived apart for a continuous period of at least five years immediately preceding the application (this is referred to as "5 years' separation").
(d) That the respondent has deserted the applicant for a continuous period of at least two years immediately preceding the making of the application.

Section 44(2) provides that the court must inquire as far as possible into the facts alleged by the applicant and any facts put forward by the respondent. The court may not hold that the civil partnership has broken down irretrievably unless the applicant satisfies the court of one or more of the facts set out in ss.(5). But if the court is satisfied of any of those facts it must make a dissolution order unless it is satisfied on all the evidence that the civil partnership has not broken down irretrievably.

There are provisions similar to **M.C.A.** for six months reconciliation and defence of grave hardship after five years separation.

N.B. Adultery is not one of the grounds.

THE HUMAN RIGHTS ACT 1998

With effect from October 2, 2000, the Human Rights Act 1998 (**H.R.A.**) incorporated the Convention for the Protection of Human Rights and Fundamental Freedoms (1950) (the Convention) into our domestic law. Thus, our law is now interpreted so that it is compatible with the **Convention**, though Parliament is not bound to change statutes which are found to be incompatible.

There are a number of articles applicable to family law and these will be discussed in the chapters relevant to them. Article 12 gives the right to marry and found a family, but it does not mention divorce or termination, so our divorce law is unaffected by the **H.R.A.**

JUDICIAL SEPARATION

Most people whose marriages have broken down will proceed to divorce. There are some, however, who do not wish to terminate the marriage, for example, because of religious objections. Nevertheless, such people often require some recognition of the breakdown and a decree of judicial separation can fill this need. It does not terminate the marriage: it simply relieves the petitioner of the duty to cohabit with the respondent (s.18(1) of the **M.C.A.**)

Others will institute proceedings for judicial separation not because they want a decree for its own sake but because they wish to obtain one of the very wide financial orders that the court can make once a decree of judicial separation has been made. Such wide orders, made under s.24 of the **M.C.A.** are only possible after a decree of nullity or divorce or judicial separation. It may be impossible for some people to obtain either of the first two mentioned decrees or they simply may not yet be ready to apply for a decree that terminates the marriage.

The grounds for judicial separation

By s.17(1) of the **M.C.A.**, there are five grounds and they correspond exactly with the five facts for divorce created by s.1(2) of the **M.C.A.** There is no need to establish that the marriage has irretrievably broken down.

Bars, defences and delays to judicial separation

Bars There is no time bar on the presentation of a petition for judicial separation. Theoretically, parties can marry on one day and then one of them can present a petition for judicial separation the next. Given that the grounds for judicial separation are the same as the facts for divorce, if a person is able to petition for the former but not the latter, it will usually be because of the absence of a time bar on the former.

However, the provisions of s.2 of the **M.C.A.** (relating to the parties having lived with each other) apply equally to proceedings for judicial separation.

Defences A respondent to a petition for judicial separation may defend upon the basis that the ground does not exist, but the defence of grave financial or other hardship is not available.

Delays The provisions of s.41 of the **M.C.A.** (relating to protection for the children) apply to proceedings for judicial separation. Thus, even where one of the grounds are proved, a court can delay a decree of judicial separation by directing that it should not be granted without further order (as a decree of judicial separation is granted in one stage, not two, it is the decree itself that is delayed). As with divorce, in practice, the decree will be withheld until such time as the court is able to exercise its **C.A.** powers or until such time as it can be persuaded that the circumstances are no longer exceptional.

Section 10 of the **M.C.A.** does not apply to judicial separation proceedings.

. . . .

NULLITY

The third type of decree that the divorce court can grant is one of nullity. As can be gathered from the word, such a decree declares the marriage to be null and void which is different from terminating it. The distinction is subtle, but important for those whose personal beliefs do not include divorce. Nevertheless, a decree of nullity ends the marriage in the same way as divorce, in the sense that the parties to it are free to marry thereafter. Less than half a per cent of petitions presented are petitions for nullity. Therefore the subject will be only briefly discussed.

Void and voidable marriages

A void marriage is one that was never a marriage at all, right from the day of its apparent celebration. As a result, at law, it is not necessary for the parties to a void marriage to obtain a decree of nullity before they are entitled to act as single people. (They usually do however: the court's powers to grant financial relief under ss.23 and 24 of the **M.C.A.** (see Ch.2) are available only where a decree has been granted.)

A voidable marriage, on the other hand, is a valid marriage until annulled by decree. As a result, the parties to such a marriage must obtain a decree before they are entitled to behave as single people.

The grounds for nullity Section 11 of the **M.C.A.** details the grounds that are available for declaring a marriage void. They are:

(a) that the parties are within the prohibited degrees. The prohibitions are based on "consanguinity" (related by blood) or "affinity" (related by marriage). In the former category, a man may not marry his mother, daughter, grandmother, granddaughter, sister, aunt or niece. In the second category, a spouse can marry into his former spouse's family (e.g. his sister-in-law) however his first marriage was terminated. A former spouse may marry stepdaughter or step-granddaughter, step-mother or step-grandmother provided that both are over 21 and the younger was never a child of the family. Spouses may also marry their daughter- in-law or mother-in-law provided that both are over 21 and both their spouses are dead;

(b) that it is not a valid marriage under the Marriage Acts 1949–1994;

Dukali v Lamrani (2012)
A marriage ceremony conducted at the Moroccan Consulate did not comply with the Marriage Act formalities; and
El Gamal v Al Maktoum (2012)
The parties had taken part in a ceremony in secret with complete absence of writing. There was no compliance with any of the formalities of the Marriage Acts and it was held in both cases to be a "Non marriage" The significance of these decisions is that, unlike void marriages, no relief is available under the **M.C.A.**

(c) that at the time of the marriage either party was already lawfully married;

(d) that the parties are not respectively male and female;

CORBETT V CORBETT (1970)

April Ashley had been born male but had undergone a complete sex change. She was treated as female by social security and by the passport authorities but the HL held that our gender is determined at birth and cannot be changed.

Numerous cases followed, culminating in HL in *Bellinger v Bellinger* (2003) declaring the law incompatible with the **H.R.A.** As a result the Gender Recognition Act (2009) **G.R.A.** was passed, providing transsexual people with legal recognition in their acquired gender subject to conditions. Legal recognition follows from the issue of a full gender recognition certificate by a Gender Recognition Panel.

In practical terms, legal recognition will have the effect that, for example, a male-to-female transsexual person will be legally recognised as a woman in English law and will be able to marry someone of the opposite gender to his or her acquired gender.

Note also that the **C.P.A.** (see later) will have some impact on this section.

(e) that either party was under the age of 16; and

(f) in the case of a polygamous marriage entered into outside England and Wales, that either party was at the time of the marriage domiciled in England and Wales.

(g) that an interim gender recognition certificate under the **G.R.A.** has, after the time of the marriage, been issued to either party to the marriage.

(h) that the respondent is a person whose gender at the time of the marriage had become the acquired gender under the **G.R.A.**

The ground most used by petitioners for annulment of a void marriage is that, at the date of its celebration, one of the parties was already lawfully married. Proof of a prior, subsisting, valid marriage at the date of celebration of the "marriage" under consideration is enough. Unlike the criminal law of bigamy, the state of the parties' knowledge or belief concerning the existence or validity of the prior marriage is irrelevant.

Section 12 of the **M.C.A.** details the six grounds that are available for declaring a marriage voidable. They are:

(a) non-consummation of marriage due to the incapacity of either party;

(b) non-consummation of marriage due to the wilful refusal of the respondent;

(c) lack of valid consent to the marriage by either party;

(d) that either party was suffering from mental disorder;

(e) that the respondent was suffering from VD in a communicable form at the time of the marriage; and

(f) that the respondent was pregnant by someone other than the petitioner at the time of the marriage.

The grounds most used by petitioners for annulment of a voidable marriage are those relating to non-consumation (which are often pleaded together, in the alternative).

The concept of non-consummation of a marriage is the same, whatever the reason alleged. Consummation is achieved by one act of sexual intercourse after the marriage ceremony. The required act of sexual intercourse must be "ordinary and complete and not partial and imperfect", so that a husband who can sustain an erection for only a very short period of time has been found incapable of consummating his marriage (*W. v W.* (HC 1967)). However, lack of ability to ejaculate, withdrawal prior to ejaculation, and the use of a condom have generally been held not to bar a finding of consummation.

If it is alleged that non-consummation is due to incapacity, it does not matter whether the reason for the incapacity is physical or psychological. However, it must be "incurable" in the sense that it is literally incurable, or curable only by an operation that is dangerous, unlikely to succeed or refused by the party suffering the incapacity.

Non-consummation due to incapacity of either party is what is required: thus a spouse could petition upon the grounds of his own incapacity.

Knowledge of the incapacity prior to the ceremony, whether it be knowledge of one's own incapacity or that of the other party, is not automatically a bar to a petition but it may well be taken into account under s.13 of the **M.C.A.** (see below).

If it is alleged that non-consummation is due to wilful refusal, the respondent's decision must be "settled and definite ... and come to without just excuse" (*Horton v Horton* (HC 1974)). Note, the wilful refusal of the respondent must be proved before a decree will be granted on this ground.

Bars, defences and delays to nullity

Bars and defences As void marriages are marriages that never existed, there can be no bar or defence to a petition for nullity relating to them (save to establish that the ground does not in fact exist).

Section 13 of the **M.C.A.** deals with bars and defences to petitions alleging marriages to be voidable.

First, a decree must be refused if the respondent satisfies the court that the petitioner by his conduct made the respondent believe that he would not petition for nullity and that it would be unjust to the respondent to grant the decree. The respondent's belief must be reasonably held and the petitioner must have known that he had the grounds to petition for a nullity decree. An example of these principles is to be found in:

> D v D (HC 1979)
> The petitioners agreeing to the adoption of a child by the parties was held to be conduct that led the respondent to believe that the petitioner would not petition for nullity. However, as the respondent wanted the decree too, there was held to be no injustice to her in granting one.

Other defences and bars are detailed in s.13 of the **M.C.A.** but these do not relate to petitions relying on non-consummation.

Delays The provisions of s.41 of the **M.C.A.** (relating to protection for children), apply to all proceedings for nullity, no matter whether it is alleged that the marriage is void or voidable.

Void Civil Partnerships
Section 49 of the **C.P.A.** sets out the grounds on which civil partnership are void:

(a) that the partners were not of the same sex;
(b) that the formal requirements necessary to register the civil partnership were not followed, if both civil partners were aware of the breach at the time of the registration;
(c) if the civil partnership document is void because one of the intended civil partners is a child (under the age of 18) and the issue of the civil partnership document has been forbidden by a person whose consent is required for the child to form a civil partnership;
(d) that the parties were within the prohibited degrees as laid down by the **C.P.A.**

Voidable Civil Partnerships
Section 50 of the **C.P.A.** sets out the following grounds:

(a) Either of the civil partners did not validly consent to the formation of the civil partnership, through a mistake, due to duress, unsoundness of mind or otherwise.
(b) At the time of the formation of the civil partnership either of the civil

partners, was suffering from a mental disorder which made them unfitted for civil partnership.

(c) One of the civil partners was pregnant other than by the applicant, but the court may not make a nullity order unless it is satisfied that the applicant did not know of the pregnancy at the time of the formation of the civil partnership. An application on this ground is subject to a six month time limit.

(d) An interim gender recognition certificate under the **G.R.A.** has been issued to either civil partner after the time of the formation of the civil partnership.

(e) The respondent is a person whose gender at the time of the formation of the civil partnership had become the acquired gender but the court may not make a nullity order unless it is satisfied that the applicant did not know at the time of the formation of the civil partnership that his or her partner had changed gender.

Section 51: Bars to relief

(1) provides that the court must not make a nullity order on the grounds that a civil partnership is voidable if the respondent satisfies the court that the applicant acted towards the respondent in such a way as to indicate that he or she would not apply for a nullity order, and that it would be unjust to the respondent to make the order now.

In most cases an application for a nullity order on the grounds that a civil partnership is voidable must be made within three years from the date that the civil partnership was formed although the court may allow later applications where it is just to do so on the basis that the applicant suffered from mental disorder at some time during the three-year period.

The failed Family Law Act 1996, Pt II

There is no question that our divorce law is unsatisfactory. The Law Commission in "Facing the Future" Law Com No.170 found that the Divorce Reform Act 1969 had failed to remove bitterness, distress and humiliation from divorce: the law is confusing and did nothing to save marriages. If felt that there was "overwhelming support" for no fault divorce. The then Government accepted the proposals in principle, but with a stormy passage through Parliament, the **F.L.A.** suffered many amendments before it received the Royal Assent in October 1997. The implementation of Pt II, which dealt with divorce reform, was postponed and postponed, during which time pilot schemes for "Information Meetings" were carried out. Under the **F.L.A.** a divorce petition could not be presented unless the parties had attended such a meeting, the purpose of which was to explain the divorce process and its consequences, and also to inform the parties about the availability of mediation and counselling.

The results of the pilot scheme showed that the public would want legal advice more than ever (completely against the basis of the reforms) and caused the Lord Chancellor to abandon Pt II.

Many MPs, practitioners and academics forecast the failure of Pt II: a basic principle was that all marriages could be saved; the petition would state that the marriage had irretrievably broken down with no reasons given and even the "guilty party" (using current terminology) able to present it. There had to be a period of one year for reflection and consideration but little thought seemed to have been given as to where and how that may take place, and the emphasis throughout was on mediation to the exclusion of legal advice.

A proposed reform to require financial and children's matters to be resolved before the decree could be granted might have been added to and thus improved the **M.C.A.** but it fell with the rest of Pt II.

FAMILY JUSTICE REVIEW

The Government announced this month that it will implement almost all of the review recommendations, published in 2011. Draft legislation was tabled in September 2012 (the draft Bill 2012) and should be implemented by 2013.

The key proposals are:

- To appoint a judge (RYDER J.) to lead up reforms;
- To allow administrators (Court Clerks) to grant decrees in undefended divorces, thus freeing judges to deal with Court work;
- Introduce a single Family Court;
- Mediation in ancillary relief matters;
- Likewise in private law children cases;
- Residence and contact to be abolished and replaced by Children arrangement Orders (see Ch.7);
- Statutory time limit of six months to be introduced in Care proceedings (see Ch.8).

N.B. Legal Aid to be removed from all Family proceedings except where domestic violence is involved.

You should by now know and understand:

- **the grounds for divorce and the five facts**
- **the grounds for terminating a civil partnership**
- **how a marriage can become annulled**

QUESTION AND ANSWER

The Question

1. Shirley was born a man and underwent complete sex change therapy and surgery in her early 20s. She met Rodney, who was unaware of these facts and they married a year later. After an unhappy two years, Shirley met Anne and embarked on a lesbian relationship with her. They went through a ceremony of marriage at their local (licensed) evangelical church.

Their relationship breaks down after a few months, culminating in Shirley hitting Anne with a beer bottle and physically ejecting her from the house.

Advise Anne, who wishes to terminate the relationship and return to live in the house in place of Shirley.

Suggested Answer

Shirley is a transsexual, and unless he has a gender regulation certificate under the **G.R.A.**, retains the gender of birth, in this case, male. Therefore, Shirley's marriage to Rodney is void ab initio. It is not necessary to obtain a decree of nullity, so both parties are free to marry someone else. The fact that Shirley and Anne have a lesbian relationship is not a bar to them marrying because legally they are of the opposite sex.

Anne has two alternative courses of action:

(i) to divorce her on the behaviour ground (s.1(2)(b) of the **M.C.A.**) citing the violent attack but she cannot petition until the first anniversary of the wedding; or

(ii) to petition for nullity on the grounds that neither party are capable of consummation (s.12 of the **M.C.A.**), though there is the potential s.13 bar that her conduct led the other to believe she would not petition for nullity. Anne can apply for an occupation order under **F.L.A.** pending a full resolution of property matters in ancillary relief proceedings.

MATRIMONIAL HOME RIGHTS, FINANCIAL AND PROPERTY AWARDS— SPOUSES

INTRODUCTION

This chapter relates to partners who are or who have been married to each other or who have registered their partnership under the **C.P.A.** Care should be taken to note whether the rights discussed relate only to married partners or to those who have been married as well. Although often referred to as "Ancillary relief", being ancillary to divorce proceedings, because of the special procedure, the division of family property and assets is usually the main consideration of the divorcing parties. It is the only grounds for litigation between them.

It is necessary to consider:

1. The rights of the respective parties to occupy the matrimonial home;
2. The range of orders available to the court;
3. The matters taken into account by the court when deciding on the division of family property.

MATRIMONIAL HOME RIGHTS—THE FAMILY LAW ACT 1996

Nowadays, many matrimonial homes are owned jointly by the spouses, both as to the legal and beneficial estate. As beneficial owners, both will have the right to occupy the home and as legal owners, both will be able to ensure that their right of occupation is not prejudiced without their consent, for any sale or mortgage requires their signature.

However, some homes are vested solely in the name of one of the parties. At common law, even though the whole of the legal and beneficial estate in the home was vested in the husband, the wife, as wife, had a right to occupy it. However, this right could be defeated by a sale or mortgage to a third party. Further, husbands did not have equal rights in homes belonging to their wives. Finally, even if a spouse had a beneficial interest in the home, if she had no share in the legal estate, it could prove very difficult to protect her interest and the attached right of occupation.

By s.30 of the **F.L.A.**, where one spouse (the owning spouse) has a right to occupy property that is or was the matrimonial home and the other (the non-owning spouse) has not, the other is given "matrimonial home rights" in that property.

Basically, "the matrimonial home rights" are:

(a) if the non-owner is in occupation of the home, the right not to be evicted from it without leave of the court; and

(b) if the non-owner is not in occupation of the home, the right to resume occupation with leave of the court.

Figure 3: Matrimonial Home Rights

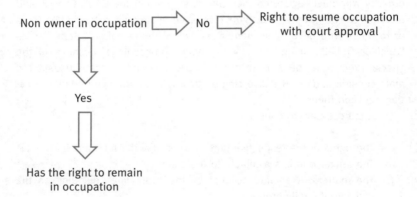

It will be noted that a spouse only receives the benefit of the Act if she needs it. A spouse who already has rights of occupation is not entitled to the statutory rights. Section 30(9) of the **F.L.A.** specifically provides that a spouse who only has an equitable interest in the home and not a legal estate, is to be treated as not being entitled to occupy the house by virtue of that interest. This is of some significance when seeking Occupation Orders. (See Ch.5.)

The rights exist until the termination of the marriage, for example by death or divorce (unless extended by the court by application made during the marriage). The rights can also be terminated or restricted by an earlier court order under s.33(5) of the **F.L.A.** This power is most often used in cases of domestic violence and will be discussed in Ch.6. Creation of rights of occupation as between spouses is not the only objective achieved by the

F.L.A. The rights are a charge on the home and can be protected against third parties. The non-owning spouse must register matrimonial home rights as either a land charge, class F (for unregistered land) or a notice (for registered land). Such registration can be effected whether or not the non-owning spouse is actually in occupation. If this is done, then any subsequent purchaser for value will take subject to the matrimonial home rights. It should be noted, however, that he then has the same right as the owning spouse to apply to the court for termination or restriction of the matrimonial home rights and his own circumstances, as well as the spouses, can be taken into account.

> KASHMIR KAUR V GILL (CA 1988)
> The court at first instance refused to enforce a wife's statutory rights of occupation against the purchaser of the home, even though she had registered a notice. In reaching this decision, the court had taken into account the purchaser's circumstances, i.e. that he was blind and wanted the property as it was convenient.
>
> **Held:** the purchaser's circumstances could be taken into account.

FINANCIAL AND PROPERTY AWARDS—THE MATRIMONIAL CAUSES ACT 1973 ANCILLARY TO DECREE PROCEEDINGS

Introduction

Following a pilot scheme in some regions, a new Ancillary relief system was introduced in June 2000. In brief, the parties are required to attend a hearing before a District Judge within 10–14 weeks of the commencement of the application. During that time a form (Form E) has to be completed which sets out the parties' income assets and outgoings and liabilities. At the hearing, the judge will highlight contentious issues, which then go to a Financial Dispute Resolution hearing. Outstanding issues should be resolved so that at a Final Hearing orders can be made. At all stages, the emphasis is on openness of disclosure and assessment of costs.

The procedure brings the proceedings into line with Lord Woolf's reforms in other areas of civil litigation.

Orders for the benefit of spouses

Nature and duration of orders By ss.23 and 24 of the **M.C.A.** the court can grant one or more of a variety of orders against either spouse for the benefit of the other:

Figure 4: Orders available under s.23 and s.24

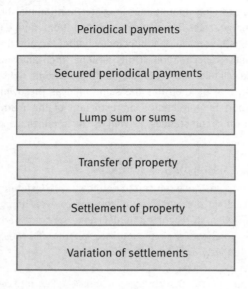

| Periodical payments |
| Secured periodical payments |
| Lump sum or sums |
| Transfer of property |
| Settlement of property |
| Variation of settlements |

(a) a periodical payments order;
(b) a secured periodical payments order;
(c) an order for lump sum or sums;
(d) a transfer of property order;
(e) a settlement of property order;
(f) a variation of settlement order; and
(g) an order extinguishing or reducing an interest in a settlement.

None of these orders can be made until a decree of divorce, nullity or judicial separation has been granted. Therefore, if the decree proceedings fail, no order for a spouse can be made under ss.23 and 24 of the **M.C.A.** All of these orders can be made on the grant of a decree or at any time afterwards, save that a spouse is barred from applying for any of these orders if he or she has remarried prior to the application.

We can now look at the orders in more detail.

(a) Periodical payments, secured and unsecured (s.23 of the **M.C.A.**). This is an order that one spouse should pay to the other a specific amount of money periodically, e.g. weekly or monthly. If the periodical payment is "secured!, this means that it is charged upon a piece of property owned by the paying spouse.

Once made, both forms of periodical payment can last for many years. The death of the payer automatically terminates an unsecured periodical payment: it does not have the same effect on a secured periodical payment, which can go on beyond the death of the payer, the reason being that the property upon which the payment is secured will still be in existence. The remarriage or death of the recipient automatically terminates both forms of periodical payment.

Apart from automatic termination, the court itself has the power to control the duration of both forms of periodical payment. It can order the payments to be made for only a specific length of time and, in addition, can direct that at the end of the specified period the recipient should not be entitled to ask for an extension of the period. (Indeed, the court can order that there should be no periodical payment at all and again, in addition, direct that the applicant should not be entitled to seek such an order at any time in the future.)

(b) Lump sum (s.23 of the **M.C.A.**). This is an order that one spouse pays the other a fixed sum or sums of money. It can be provided that the lump sum should be paid in one go or by specified instalments. If the lump sum is ordered to be paid in instalments, the instalments can be secured on some property owned by the payer.

(c) Transfer of property (s.24 of the **M.C.A.**). This is an order that one spouse transfer to the other property to which the former is entitled.

"Property" is not defined in the **M.C.A.** and s.24 has been used to transfer items such as furniture, jewellery, cars, and other tangible items. It can also cover stocks and shares and, most important, land, including the matrimonial home. Even if the matrimonial home is mortgaged, it can be the subject of a transfer order, and likewise if it is rented (save for a statutory tenancy under the Rent Acts).

(d) Settlement of property order and variation of settlement order (s.24 of the **M.C.A.**). The former is an order that one spouse settle property to which he is entitled for the benefit of the other. There are no restrictions on the type of settlement that the court can create and again property is widely interpreted.

The variation of settlement order is an order that any ante- or post-nuptial settlement made on the spouses should be varied for their benefit. The phrase "ante- or post-nuptial settlement" conjures up pictures of the sort of arrangements entered into in bygone days by members of the landed gentry on the marriage of their children. Fortunately, the phrase has been widely interpreted and also covers a matrimonial home bought by the parties in their joint names.

By using these two orders the courts have been able to create very sophisticated arrangements designed to meet the needs of individual cases. Two examples will suffice to illustrate how wide-ranging the orders can be.

MESHER V MESHER (CA 1980)
The home was in joint names, on the usual trust for sale. The court varied the settlement by providing that the property should not be sold until the youngest child of the family reached 17 and in the meantime, the wife should have exclusive rights of occupation.

E. v E. (Financial Provision) (1990)
A wealthy father had created a substantial discretionary trust for his son, his wife and their children, as well as making other provisions for them. The wife was extravagant and profligate and after 10 years of marriage, she left for another man leaving the children with their father. The court ordered £250,000 be transferred from the trust to the wife and that the father be removed as a trustee of the settlement.

(e) An order extinguishing or reducing an interest in a settlement (s.24 of the **M.C.A.**). Such an order must relate to an interest of either spouse in an ante- or post-nuptial settlement.

Under the **H.R.A.**, art.6 states that everyone is entitled to a fair hearing by an independent tribunal, and the press may be excluded for the protection of the private live of the parties. By art.8, everyone has a right to respect for his private and family life, his home and his correspondence. Interference can only be justified, amongst other grounds, for the protection of the rights and freedom of others.

Matters taken into account when making orders By s.25(1) of the **M.C.A.**, it is provided that, when deciding whether and how to exercise its powers, the court must consider all the circumstances of the case, but give first consideration to the welfare of any minor children of the family.

Suter v Suter and Jones (CA 1986), it was held that giving "first consideration" to the welfare of the children in financial proceedings did not mean that the welfare of the child overrode all other considerations. The courts had to:

"consider all the circumstances ... always bearing in mind the important consideration of the welfare of the children and then try to attain a financial result which is just as between husband and wife."

The application of this principle is illustrative.

These provisions remain in force but were considerably affected by the *Child Support Acts* (**C.S.A.**), whereby child maintenance was assessed using rigid formulae reducing substantially the jurisdiction of the courts. Now, the emphasis is on parents reaching agreement so the **M.C.A.** could regain some importance. Chapter 4 contains a more detailed discussion of these provisions.

Section 25(2) of the **M.C.A.** directs the court to have regard to a list of factors when exercising their powers to make financial provision for a spouse. In *Piglowska v Piglowski* (1998) the House of Lords stated that the factors did not lay down a particular order.

LANDMARK CASE

In *White v White* (2000) the HL stated that the objective of s.25 should be fairness. Lord Nicholls suggested that once housing needs of both parties had been met, there should be a "notional yardstick of equality" when dividing the remaining matrimonial property and Assets.

KEY CASES

McFARLANE v McFARLANE AND MILLER v MILLER (2006)
These two cases were heard together in another landmark ruling by HC. The decisions have far reaching effects on ancillary relief proceedings. Their Lordships followed *White v White* but said that fairness is an elusive concept.

"[But] fairness generates obligations as well as rights. The financial provision made on divorce ... is not a case of 'taking away' from one party and 'giving' to the other property which 'belongs' to the former. Each party to a marriage is entitled to a fair share of the available property."

The requirements of fairness have to be looked at in each particular case.

HC were also at pains to stress that settlements may well include a compensation element aimed at redressing any significant prospective economic disparity between the parties arising from the way they conducted their marriage.

In *McFarlane*, for example, the wife had agreed with the husband to give up her career as a solicitor and stay at home to raise the three children of the marriage. The marriage lasted 16 years. Their arrangement greatly advantaged the husband in terms of his earning capacity but left the wife severely handicapped so far as her own earning capacity was concerned.

"The wife suffers a double loss: a diminution in her earning capacity and the loss of a share in her husband's enhanced income. Although less marked than in the past, women may still suffer a disproportionate financial loss on the breakdown of a marriage because of their traditional role as home-maker and child-carer."

One of the problems in *McFarlane* was that although they had a large income their capital was virtually exhausted by housing the parties, so that a clean break was not applicable. However, the HC saw no difficulty in awarding periodical payments to the wife.

"It would be extraordinary if, where necessary, the court could not order the advantaged party to pay compensation to the other out of his enhanced earnings".

This principle is applicable as much to short marriages as to long marriages.

Figure 5: The specified matters

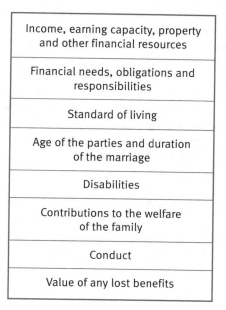

Income, earning capacity, property and other financial resources
Financial needs, obligations and responsibilities
Standard of living
Age of the parties and duration of the marriage
Disabilities
Contributions to the welfare of the family
Conduct
Value of any lost benefits

Each of the matters in s.25(1) are of equal value and must be considered in turn.

(a) Income, earning capacity, property and other financial resources. The court must have regard to all of the income and capital of both parties, including any they are likely to have in the foreseeable future. So far as income is concerned, this will include both earned and unearned income, e.g. wages, salary, profits from a business, bonuses, commissions and overtime, dividends and interest from investments and pensions. So far as capital is concerned this will include all land, investments, cash, and personal possessions even if obtained as a bequest or gift or meant for a specific purpose, such as compensation. Its source or purpose will be borne in mind, however, and the court will not always make an order that divests the owner of any benefit.

In *McFarlane* it was said that in the case of a short marriage fairness may well require that the claimant should not be entitled to a share of the other's "non-matrimonial property". The source of the assets may be taken into account but its importance will diminish over time. Put the other way round, the court is expressly required to take into account the duration of the marriage. If the assets are not "family assets", or not generated by the joint efforts of the parties, then the duration of the marriage may justify a departure from the yardstick of equality of division.

In *Miller v Miller*, the husband received £20 million from the sale of a company that he had built up. At the end of their three-year marriage, she was awarded a lump sum of £5 million.

A party's earning capacity is also a resource (including any that he is likely to have in the foreseeable future) and it is also specifically provided that the court should have regard to any increase in earning capacity which it is reasonable to expect a party to take steps to acquire. If the court thinks that such a party is being unreasonable then they can attribute "lost" income to that party. Obviously, the court will take into account such matters as job or overtime availability, the efforts made to find employment or better employment, the availability of retraining or refresher courses and the feasibility of a party undergoing such courses.

LEADBEATER V LEADBEATER (1985)

Wife, aged 47, had been a secretary before marriage but the court thought it unreasonable for her to learn new skills. However, she could have worked longer hours at her part-time job as a receptionist and her notional earnings were set at £2,550, as opposed to her actual income of £1,700.

Often the applicant is in receipt of State benefits. Do these count as a resource? If they are not means tested, e.g. child benefit—and thus will be paid whether or not a financial award is made in favour of the applicant, then they count as a resource, to be taken into account when assessing the award. However, if the state benefit is means tested, e.g. income support, family credit, this is not taken into account as a resource as a general rule. Respondents to financial applications are not generally permitted to argue that the applicant can claim a State benefit if no (or a small) financial award were made against him (but see, e.g. *Delaney v Delaney* (CA 1990)).

One or both of the parties may have a new partner, either as a new spouse or as a cohabitee, by the time the court is deciding what financial orders to make after decree. If such a new partner has their own income or capital, then such resources cannot be taken as being the resources of the party with whom they are living (but see below).

(b) Financial needs, obligations and responsibilities. Again, prima facie, the court must have regard to all such matters, including those which the parties are likely to have in the foreseeable future. This obviously includes living expenses, e.g. mortgage or rent, council tax, water rates, electricity and gas, food and clothing. Regard will also be had to income tax and social security contributions, to union dues and pension contributions and to the cost of travelling to and from work.

The parties will be expected to be reasonable when giving evidence of such matters and not to inflate their needs in the hope that the court will take the view that there is less available for division or more needed. Thus constant wining and dining, expensive holidays abroad and powerful and expensive motor cars would not be regarded as a part of the needs of an ordinary person. Even some of the matters that are referred to above, e.g. pension contributions, could be disregarded as unreasonable if their size made them so in the circumstances.

Any liabilities of a capital nature must also be taken into account. For example, when assessing the value of the matrimonial home, the outstanding mortgage, if any, must be deducted. Liabilities, such as a bank overdraft, personal or for business purposes, must be taken into account. Tax that will have to be paid on the realisation of investments must not be forgotten.

As was mentioned above, by the time the court decides what orders to make after decree, either or both of the parties may have a new partner, and that new partner may have an income of his own. While such a resource is not a resource of the party to the proceedings, the fact that his partner has an income will be taken into account to the extent that the partner contributes to, and thereby reduces, the needs of the party. The position becomes more complex when the new partner can afford to contribute but does not do so. Sometimes, such a partner will be taken as contributing a reasonable amount. As has been seen, in *Suter v Suter and Jones*, the court made an order that left the wife without enough money to meet all her needs, assuming the co-respondent would start contributing to the household expenses.

On the other hand, the new partner may, reasonably, have no income or capital to contribute. In such cases, the question then is whether the party to the proceedings is entitled to have taken into account as an obligation or responsibility the needs of his new partner. Such cases usually arise where the husband has a new partner, by whom he has children or who already has children of her own. While such children are not the first consideration of the court (see above), they, and their mother, are to be seen as the responsibility of the husband.

(c) Standard of living. The court must take into account the standard of living enjoyed by the family before the breakdown of the marriage. In some cases the court will exercise its powers so that the marriage breakdown will have the least possible effect on the standard of living of the parties.

(d) Age of the parties and duration of the marriage. The age of the parties must be taken into account by the court and can be relevant for several reasons. For example, the age of a person may affect promotion prospects or, more radically, whether or not a job can be found at all. See *M. v M. (Financial Provision)* (1987).

The duration of the marriage must also be taken into account by the court. There is no definition of what is "long" or "short", but a "short marriage" is usually taken to mean one of only a very few years. Generally, the parties to a short marriage will have less claim on each other than those who have been married for some appreciable period, on the basis that they will have changed their positions less drastically.

> **ATTAR V ATTAR (1985)**
> Before marriage to a multi-millionaire, she had been an air hostess earning £15,000 p.a. The marriage only lasted six months: she was awarded a lump sum of £30,000.

But in *Miller* (above) the HC were prepared to award a lump sum to a wife after a three-year marriage where the husband had made substantial profits during the marriage, although the amount given to her was well short of equal division.

Even a short marriage can produce children, and short marriages between older couples can still mean a change in their positions, for example the loss of pension rights previously accrued.

(e) Disabilities. The court must take into account any physical or mental disability of either of the parties to the marriage. In practice, the needs are usually addressed under headings (a) and (b).

(f) Contributions to the welfare of the family. It is specifically provided that this includes any contribution made by looking after the home or caring for the family. Thus the wife, who gives up her job and contributes nothing to the family in hard cash, but is the home maker and child rearer, has the value of such activities recognised. The House of Lords emphasised this point in *White v White* and stated that there should be no discrimination on financial grounds between the earner on the one hand and "the homemaker", who stayed at home looking after the house and children, on the other.

McFarlane v McFarlane re-emphasised this point even going so far as to say that the division of property may include a compensation element where the party who had stayed at home had given up a career to do so.

(g) Conduct. The court must take into account the conduct of each of the parties *"whatever the nature of the conduct and whether it occurred during the marriage or after the separation or dissolution or annulment of the marriage"* if in the court's opinion it would be inequitable to ignore it. The words in italics were added by Sch.8 to the Family Law Act 1996 after MPs had made it clear that they felt insufficient weight was given to conduct by the courts. In *Wachtel v Wachtel* (CA 1973), Lord Denning M.R. had said that the courts should only take conduct into account where it was "obvious and gross". According to this formula, there had to be a certain amount of extremity, which in past cases has included such conduct as stabbing or shooting one's spouse.

Further, in *K. v K.* (HC 1990), the court stated that:

> "the court is entitled to look at the whole of the picture, including the conduct during the marriage and after the marriage, which may or may not have contributed to the breakdown ... or which in some other way makes it inequitable to ignore the conduct of each of the parties."

Miller v Miller confirmed that there must be extremity of conduct and the HC were critical of the CA for taking conduct into account in a fairly straight forward example of a short marriage breaking down. In the following cases, the spouses' claim for ancillary relief was affected by their conduct.

KYTE V KYTE (CA 1988)

The wife behaved callously when the husband, a manic depressive, made two suicide attempts. On the first, she was present and only called assistance at the last moment: on the second she encouraged him, giving him the tablets and alcohol with which to kill himself and jeering him when he failed to carry out his intentions. The court found as a fact that the wife wanted the husband dead so that she could inherit his money, and share it with her lover.

EVANS V EVANS (CA 1989)

The wife had been convicted of soliciting others to murder the husband.

LEADBEATER V LEADBEATER (1985)

The conduct of both parties cancelled each other out so that it ceased to be an issue in the case.

(h) The value of any lost benefits. In divorce and nullity cases, the court must take into account the value of any benefit the parties lose the chance of acquiring, most notably, pension rights. In *Brooks v Brooks* (HC 1995) the court compensated the wife by leaving the pension with the husband but giving her other assets.

In relation to pensions, the courts now have three options available to them:

(a) make a variation of settlement order under s.24 of the **M.C.A.**, as in *Brooks v Brooks*;

(b) "earmark" pensions under the Pensions Act 1995, that is, order that the Trustees or Managers of the pension fund pay a specified portion of the pension to the other spouse when it becomes payable; or

(c) "split" the pension under the Welfare Reform and Pensions Act 1999. This means that a specific portion of the accrued pension fund is allocated to the other spouse immediately. The parties can then make their own contributions to their fund as they see fit.

In *T v T* (1998) it was said that these orders are at the court's discretion and they were not bound to deal with pensions, even if there was a fund, if other satisfactory provision could be made, e.g. by lump sum or periodical payment orders.

In addition to the list of factors just discussed, there are further considerations for the courts. There is contained in s.25A of the **M.C.A.**, a section that was introduced by the Matrimonial and Family Proceedings Act 1984 (**M.F.P.A.**) and which embodies the policy decision that the objective for the exercise of the court's financial powers should be to make the parties financially independent of each other. This principle is often referred to as the clean break principle. It applies only where the court has granted a decree of divorce or nullity.

LEGISLATION HIGHLIGHTER

By s.25A(1), the court is placed under a duty to consider whether it is appropriate to make orders that will terminate the parties' financial obligations towards each other as soon after the decree as the court thinks is just and reasonable. The court must therefore consider whether it should make use of the powers it has to make no orders for continuing provision (primarily periodical payments) and to ensure that no future applications are made. Only if such a situation is created can the parties be said to be truly independent of each other.

Section 25A(2) creates a secondary obligation on the court. If it has decided that an order for periodical payments should be made (thus not ordering a clean break), then it must consider whether to order that the payments should cease after a specified period, a period designed to permit an adjustment to financial independence without undue hardship.

It must be emphasised that the court has no duty to order a clean break, immediate or delayed: it has a duty to consider whether it should order a clean break in every case where it was asked to exercise its financial powers on divorce (or nullity).

The exercise of the powers The first point to make is that the court can make one or more of the orders specified in ss.23 and 24 of the **M.C.A.** In other words, by a judicious combination of orders drawn from both sections, the court can create a "package deal" that is suitable for the particular couple. It is therefore somewhat unrealistic to consider when any particular order will be made, in isolation: when circumstances permit, a generous periodical payments order might be reflected in the capital award or disposition of the home, and vice versa. Further, orders may be made in favour of both of the parties: e.g. if circumstances permit, the court may prefer to order the transfer of the home outright to the wife coupled with an order that she pay the husband a lump sum, instead of one of the more complex property adjustment orders. This must be borne in mind during the following discussion.

(a) The clean break. Parliament could have provided that a clean break should be ordered in every case immediately. It did not, thus showing that, although the clean break is to be the financial objective on marriage breakdown, it is also thought that a clean break will not always be appropriate. Further, Parliament has left it up to the courts to decide the sort of cases in which clean breaks are appropriate, giving them no further guidance than the principle and factors previously discussed. (But note *McFarlane v McFarlane* (above)).

Prior to the **C.S.A.**, the most problematical cases concerned women with children or women who had cared for children. Their commitments often took them out of the job market or gave them little chance of entering it. Without periodical payments, many suffered a reduction in living standards. However, practitioners realised that if the wife was to have to rely on State benefits, then income support would meet the mortgage repayments. Thus, a clean break could be effected by transferring the matrimonial home to her and the State would foot the mortgage bill. This popular clean break agreement has suffered substantive setbacks in the last few years, both from the **C.S.A.** and the Social Security legislation.

Under the **C.S.A.**, the levels of child maintenance precluded such arrangements except in very rare cases. One such example is *Mawson v Mawson* (1994):

> The couple lived together for eight years, the last three in marriage. He had a career as an officer in the R.A.F. but she had been looking after their young child. He paid child support after separation and was ordered to pay periodical payments to the wife for nine months, after which the court expected her to obtain employment so that she could maintain the matrimonial home which the husband had transferred to her.

Even if there are no children, or an agreement can be reached under the new arrangements, one has now to consider the provisions of ss.107 and 108 of the Social Security Administration Act 1992 and the Income Support (Liable Relative) Regulations 1990. There are long standing regulations permitting the D.S.S. to recover income support payments from liable relatives, but that power ceased on a decree absolute. This is no longer the case and the Department can effectively re-write a clean break settlement by proceeding against the ex-husband whenever the ex-wife and or children become dependent on income support. That legislation is clearly in conflict with the spirit of s.25A of the M.C.A.

In cases where a clean break may still be an appropriate option, the courts have to consider whether or not it is acceptable for a woman to remain financially dependent on her ex-spouse indefinitely.

WATERMAN V WATERMAN (CA 1989)
The wife was granted periodical payments order for five years, even though she had a five year old child. The judge at first instance refused to extend it. The Court of Appeal said she could apply for an extension at the end of the period but she would still have to make out a case.

ASHLEY V BLACKMAN (1988)
A clean break was imposed where husband had limited means and wife, who was on state benefits, would not suffer as a result of the loss of periodical payments. The court said it had to consider the two policies of clean break and protecting state funds and strike "whatever balance ... between them that the requirements of justice in the particular circumstances appear to dictate".

Lump sum compensation is only usually only available to more wealthy families. During the 1990s there were a series of so-called "big money" cases where wealthy husbands were ordered to pay lump sums sufficient to meet the reasonable needs of their respective wives under the second heading of the specified matters. In *Duxbury v Duxbury* (1990) the husband's advisers produced a sophisticated computer programme for calculating how this figure might be arrived at. It became widely used. In *Gojkovic v Gojkovic* (1990) and *Conran v Conran* (1997) the wives were awarded more because of their "outstanding" and "exceptional" contributions to their husbands' businesses. Although the sums awarded were large (£9.5 million in one case and over £10 million in *Conran*), they still represented only a small proportion of the husband's wealth.

The House of Lords in *White v White* were critical of this approach.

White v White. HC said there had been too much emphasis on reasonable needs. Whilst the *Duxbury* calculation was a "useful tool" it only arrived at her reasonable needs. All the specified matters should be considered to arrive at a fair result, especially resources and contributions. In respect of the latter, there should be no discrimination between the wealth producer and the "homemaker". Where there is a surplus after both parties' reasonable needs have been met, the judge should consider equality of division as a yardstick and depart from it only if there is good reason to do so.

Despite these comments, their Lordships refused to overrule the award of the CA giving less than half to the wife, largely because of the contributions made to the family business by the husband's father.

Following *White v White*, the CA in *Cowan v Cowan* (2002) awarded the wife 37 per cent of the family fortune because the husband had made a "stellar contribution" and had shown the "Midas touch" in setting up and expanding their business, but in *L v L* (2002) the CA did award 50 per cent of the assets to the wife. Both were "big money" cases and the effect of *White* on couples of lesser means is still not clear.

(b) Income awards. In *Wachtel v Wachtel* (CA 1973) Lord Denning M.R. stated that as a starting point the wife should "receive one third of the joint earnings and assets". The parties' incomes from all sources are added together and divided by three. The resulting figure is the amount of income the wife should have. If her own income does not add up to this figure, then it is to be made by a periodical payments order from the husband. This has become known as the "One third rule" for obvious reasons. However, the use of the word rule does an injustice to Lord Denning who did stress the principle should be a starting point only. Once a figure for periodical payments is arrived at using the one third rule, the court then considers whether it is appropriate.

This rule is only really relevant today in cases where there is only one earning spouse but even then it probably has to be tempered with *White v White* fairness.

A more sophisticated principle for calculating periodical payments is known as the "Net Effect Method" and was first fully stated by Ormrod J. in *Stockford v Stockford* (1981). The court arrives at a proposed order (whether by using the one third rule or by any other means) and then calculates what the parties respective positions would be if the proposed order were made. The calculations must include all income relevant for s.25 of the **M.C.A.**, bearing in mind the reduction of the payer's income by the proposed order, and takes account of reasonable expenditure that the parties have, particularly tax and expenses for earning it, but also including revised housing and living costs. What is left is the respective spendable incomes which can then be adjusted through the order to achieve the result which the court thinks is most appropriate.

It should also be noted that the court will not generally make a periodical payments order which will reduce the payer's income below "subsistence level" (see *Allen v Allen* (1986)). Subsistence level is the amount which the D.S.S. would find the payer entitled to if he were on income support and housing benefit.

(c) Capital awards. The one third rule, as first stated in *Wachtel v Wachtel*, applied not only to the calculation of the wife's periodical payments but also to her capital claims. However, it was soon appreciated that there were many cases in which the one third rule could not be usefully used even as the starting point it was meant to be.

The result has been the development of sophisticated property adjustment orders using the court's powers to settle or vary an existing settlement of property. Typical is the case of:

> MESHER V MESHER (1973)
> The home was in joint names on the usual trust for sale. There were no other assets. An application of the one third rule would have indicated no capital award to the wife, as her joint interest in the home already exceeded her entitlement to one third. However, the court were concerned to ensure that the nine-year-old child of the marriage should be accommodated, so provided that the trust for sale should be varied and that the home should not be sold until the child reached 17 or further order.

Not surprisingly, this type of order became called "the Mesher order" and was extremely popular in the Seventies.

The advantage of the "*Mesher*" case was also its disadvantage: it put off the evil day when the wife (and possibly children) are put on the street. By 1978, particularly in *Martin v Martin*, the Court of Appeal were critical of the universal use of such orders. It was pointed out that children do not always leave home at 17, that even when they do, the wife has to find somewhere to live and she will then (in all probability) be in her forties with negligible employment prospects. Despite these comments, the introduction of the C.S.A. has seen a resurgence of *Mesher* orders, allowing absent parents to retain a capital interest in the home whilst still paying maintenance assessments in respect of the children.

They are probably likely to be even more popular following *White v*

White as it can achieve fairness to the husband (eventually) whilst housing the wife and children in the immediate term.

PRE-NUPTIAL AGREEMENTS

Have long been problematic, because basically they contravene public policy in that they undermine the sanctity of marriage. They are therefore unenforceable. Recent cases have been more relaxed about them and have upheld some agreements. Factors include:

- Did the parties understand the agreement?
- Did they have independent legal advice?
- Was any pressure applied?
- Was there abuse of a dominant position?

> **G v G (FINANCIAL PROVISION) [2004]**
> Agreement upheld despite the fact that no advice had been taken, but both parties had been previously divorced and had conducted all their affairs on a contractual basis.

> **K v K (ANCILLARY RELIEF: PRE NUPTIAL AGREEMENT) [2003]**
> The agreement had been made the day before the marriage and independent advice had been given to both parties. Although it was taken into account the wife received a higher award because of the needs of the child of the marriage who resided with her.

> **KEY CASE**
>
> **RADMACHER V GRANATINO 2010**
> By a majority of 8 to 1, the Supreme Court has taken a huge step towards recognising pre-nuptial agreements.
> From now on, the courts will give effect to a pre-nup that has been freely entered into by each party with a full appreciation of its implications unless in the circumstances prevailing it would not be fair to do so.
> The traditional rule that pre-nups are contrary to public policy has been disapproved, but it remains the case that a pre-nuptial agreement is not enforceable of itself. The parties still cannot enter into a binding contract that can preclude either side applying to the courts on divorce. The court remains the "... arbiter of the financial arrangements between the parties when it brings a marriage to an end".

> The court should give effect to pre-nup save where unfair. "A nuptial agreement cannot be allowed to prejudice the reasonable requirements of any children".

Orders for the benefit of children

Children of the family can have the same types of orders made in their favour, against either of the parties of the marriage, as can the parties themselves. For a discussion of this, see Ch.4.

Brief mention must be made of the court's powers to:

(a) order a spouse to pay maintenance pending suit to the other, a temporary periodical payment that ceases on decree absolute (s.22 of the **M.C.A.**); and

(b) order a sale of property when it has made any of the orders in ss.23 or 24 of the **M.C.A.**, save for unsecured periodical payments (s.24A of the **M.C.A.**).

FINANCIAL AWARDS—THE DOMESTIC PROCEEDINGS AND MAGISTRATES' COURTS ACT 1978

It may be the case that a party to a marriage may need some form of financial order against the other but cannot or does not wish to issue divorce proceedings.

The **D.P.M.C.A.** gives the court power to order financial relief without obtaining any order affecting the status of the marriage itself. Three different situations are covered by the Act.

Sections 1 and 2 of the D.P.M.C.A.

Although the applicant is not seeking any form of decree, he still has to establish one of the grounds as set out in s.1 before the court can grant him one of the financial orders set out in s.2. The grounds are:

(a) that the respondent has failed to provide reasonable maintenance for the applicant;

(b) that the respondent has failed to provide or make proper contribution towards the reasonable maintenance of a child of the family; and

(c) that the respondent has behaved in such a way that the applicant cannot reasonably be expected to live with him.

It will be noted that these grounds bear some similarity to the facts that evidence irretrievable breakdown of marriage, but they are not identical. The concept of behaviour is exactly the same under the **D.P.M.C.A.** as it is under the **M.C.A.**, but there is no adultery or separation ground. It is thought that the adultery of the respondent could be used as one of the elements to establish behaviour. On the other hand, s.1 of the **D.P.M.C.A.** contains aground not available in divorce proceedings, that of failure to provide reasonable maintenance. There is no definition of the term "reasonable maintenance" in the Act: clearly, the court would have to take into account the parties respective financial positions at least in making their determination.

Once the applicant has proved one of the grounds, the court has the power to make one or more of the orders as set out in s.2. They are:

(a) that the respondent should pay periodical payments to the applicant and/or a child of the family; and

(b) that the respondent should pay a lump sum to the applicant and or a child of the family, such lump sum not to exceed £1,000.

The payments for children can be ordered to be made direct to them or to some third party for their benefit.

It will be noted that the court has a far more limited range of orders available to it under the **D.P.M.C.A.** than it does under ss.23 and 24 of the **M.C.A.**

If the applicant fails to prove one of the grounds, all is not lost: the court still has the power to make the orders for the benefit of children.

Orders for periodical payments cease on the death of the payer. Orders for periodical payments to a spouse cease on her remarriage. The rules for the cessation of periodical payments for children on their reaching a certain age are the same as under the **M.C.A.** (see above). Further, orders for periodical payments that are payable to a spouse, either for herself or a child, cease if the parties continue to cohabit or resume cohabitation after the making of the order for a period of periods exceeding six months.

Once a ground is proved, the court has to decide whether to make any order at all. Again, under the **D.P.M.C.A.**, the welfare of any minor child of the family, while a minor, is the court's first consideration. Then, by s.3, the court is given a list of factors to take into account. For both spouse and child orders, the factors are virtually identical to those listed in s.25(2)(3)(4) of the **M.C.A.** What should be carefully noted is that under the **D.P.M.C.A.**, the court has no duty to consider imposing a clean break upon even the parties and cannot do so even if the parties consent.

FINANCIAL AWARDS—S.27 OF THE MATRIMONIAL CAUSES ACT 1973

The court can grant periodical payments, secured or unsecured, and lump sums for spouses and children of the family on proof simply of failure to provide reasonable maintenance. Again, s.27 provides a means of obtaining orders for financial relief without issuing decree proceedings. However, it is another provision that is little used, despite the fact that the range of orders available is wider than under the **D.P.M.C.A.**

FINANCIAL AND PROPERTY AWARDS—S.15 OF THE CHILDREN ACT 1989

Section 15 of the **C.A.** provides for the grant of a range of financial orders for the benefit of a child. The applicant must be the parent (or guardian) of the child and the orders can be made against a parent.

It must be stressed that the availability of these orders is not dependent upon the parties to the application being married to one another: it is dependent upon parenthood. Nevertheless, married parents may wish to make use of s.15 of the **C.A.**, which is yet another provision whereby the court can grant financial relief without the necessity of the parties first issuing decree proceedings.

Further, the term "parent" includes ex-spouses in relation to whom the child is a child of the family.

The nature of the orders possible under s.15 of the **C.A.** is discussed in Ch.4. By now, it will be appreciated that there are a number of jurisdictions available for the grant of financial and property awards, all bearing a similarity to each other but all having significant differences. These are not completely arbitrary; some rationale can be found when it is remembered that different situations are being catered for.

Revision Checklist

You should now know and understand:

- the types of orders that can be made in ancillary relief proceedings
- the specified matters set out in the M.C.A and the application of them
- the full range of jurisdictions which can provide financial awards

QUESTION AND ANSWER

"The first point that cannot be overemphasised too much, is that there is no rule in *White v White* ... the only universal rule is to apply the s.25(2) criteria to all the circumstances of the case and ... to arrive at a fair result that avoids discrimination." (Thorpe L.J. in *Cordle v Cordle* (2001))

Discuss

Suggested Answer

This is probably the most accurate statement of the law on ancillary relief post *White*.

You should explain the factors that the court takes into account, that is earning capacity and assets, needs and obligations, standard of living, age and duration of marriage, disabilities, contribution to the family welfare, conduct and lost benefits. It should be noted that children are a first consideration.

You should then go on to expand on *White v White* notably the principle of fairness, the "yardstick of equality" and the removal of discrimination against the homemaker's contribution to the marriage.

You should note the decisions in *McFarlane* and *Miller* in particular the use of periodical payments as compensation and their comments as to non-matrimonial property especially in relation to the duration of the marriage.

MATRIMONIAL HOME RIGHTS, FINANCIAL AND PROPERTY AWARDS— UNMARRIED PARTNERS AND SPOUSES WHO ARE NOT DIVORCING

INTRODUCTION

The previous chapter considered property rights of husband and wife in matrimonial proceedings.

This chapter relates to spouses who do not seek a decree and to partners who have never been married to each other.

In relation to the former, the following rights are important where divorce is not contemplated, or where a spouse has become insolvent or died. With cohabitees, the **Matrimonial Causes Act 1973** does not apply so these are their only rights with regard to joint property. The only difference between the two classes is that cohabitees have to prove to the court that they had a "settled" relationship which was intended to be permanent. In both cases, the parties have to rely on property law and in particular, the law of trusts.

Establishing a Trust

When dealing with land, there will always be documentary evidence as to ownership—the title deeds. It may be that both parties own the legal estate or only one. In some cases of joint legal ownership the deeds will also spell out the ownership of the equitable (beneficial) estate. More rarely, there may be a separate declaration of trust document that does this. In these cases, in the absence of fraud, the provisions for the ownership of the home are conclusive: extrinsic evidence to challenge the details in the deeds cannot be adduced (*Goodman v Gallant* (CA 1986)). The result is that the ownership dispute has been resolved solely by consideration of the title deeds.

However, in some cases of joint ownership the beneficial interests are not spelt out. Here there is a rebuttable presumption that the legal owners are each entitled to an equal share of the beneficial estate. Further, the legal estate in the home may be vested in the sole name of one of the cohabitees. In this case there is a rebuttable presumption that the beneficial interest also belongs exclusively to that person. In both these situations therefore, consideration of the title deeds alone will not necessarily provide the answer to an ownership dispute. Extrinsic evidence to rebut the presumptions can be adduced, evidence of the existence of a trust behind the deeds.

Standard works on Equity categorise trusts into four types: express, resulting, implied and constructive.

Figure 6: Types of Trust

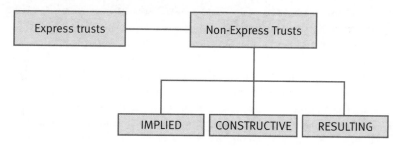

Express trusts, those created by the express declaration of the person in whom the property is vested, are not common in the family context. The traditional distinctions between the other three are of little relevance: not only do the standard works on Equity fail to agree on categorisation but the family law judges have often shown a disregard for it. What is of relevance is the circumstances in which the court will accept that a trust has arisen, whether resulting, implied or constructive.

The principles for resolving the ownership dispute will be discussed as if the property were in the sole name of the man and the woman were claiming a share, but it must be remembered that they are equally applicable where the property is vested in the sole name of the woman and where the property is in joint names, but the applicant is claiming more than the presumed half share.

Payment towards the purchase price

Where A provides the whole or part of the purchase price for property that is conveyed into B's name, there is a rebuttable presumption that A intended that he, A, should benefit and that B should hold the property on trust for A, either exclusively or in part, i.e. the beneficial estate "results" in whole or in part, to A. The trust is therefore known as a resulting trust.

The concept of resulting trust is rarely directly applicable in the family context because usually the home is not purchased outright but by way of a mortgage. However, the influence of the doctrine will be seen in the principles next discussed.

A common intention inferred from conduct

The starting point is the body of principles stated in two cases in the House of Lords, *Pettitt v Pettitt* (HC 1969) and *Gissing v Gissing* (HC 1970). Both cases concerned a spouse who did not have an interest in the legal estate in the home claiming to be entitled to a beneficial interest by way of trust.

KEY CASES

PETTITT V PETTITT AND GISSING V GISSING

Virtually all the Lords, in both cases specifically stated that a trust could arise where both parties had intended it should: the court should look for "a common intention that both parties should be beneficially entitled" (hereafter referred to as "the common intent"). Further, it would seem that the majority in both cases felt that it was necessary to be able to infer the common intention, as distinct from imputing to the parties what a reasonable person would have intended in the circumstances.

However, proof of conduct from which the court can infer the common intent is not sufficient. The woman must also prove that she has "acted to her detriment or significantly altered her position in reliance on the common intent" before a trust in her favour will arise. The necessity for such conduct was first clearly stated in *Grant v Edwards* (CA 1986), but has been confirmed by the Lords in *Lloyds Bank Plc v Rosset* (HC 1990).

Therefore, before such a trust can be established, the court will scrutinise the parties' conduct for two reasons: the first, to ascertain whether there was the common intent; and the second, to ascertain whether the woman has acted upon it. The crucial questions are then seen to be what sort of conduct will give rise to the inference of common intent and what sort of conduct will show that the woman has acted upon it?

KEY CASE

LLOYDS BANK PLC V ROSSET

Lord Bridge found that discussions between the parties as to their interests in the property do not amount to conduct from which a common intent can be inferred: presumably, nothing needs to be inferred from express discussions. What is looked for are:

> "direct contributions to the purchase price by the partner who is not the legal owner, whether initially or by payment of mortgage instalments." These "will readily justify the inference necessary to the creation of a constructive trust. But ... it is at least extremely doubtful whether anything less will do."

Lord Bridge made no comment on the sort of conduct needed to show that the woman has acted to her detriment in relying upon the common intent. Arguably, he did not need to. If she has made direct contributions to the purchase price of the property, then this will surely be taken as her having acted to her detriment in relying upon the common intent. If she has not, apparently, she will not be able to satisfy the court that an inference of common intent should be drawn and her claim will fail at this point.

An express agreement

Where there is evidence of the parties having entered into "an agreement, arrangement or understanding that the property is to be shared beneficially" then, in some circumstances, the court will hold that a trust has arisen. The finding of such an agreement, etc. can only be based on evidence of "express discussions" between the parties, however "imperfectly remembered and however imprecise the terms". All the above principles are stated in the judgment of Lord Bridge in *Lloyd's Bank Plc v Rosset*.

However, proving such an agreement, etc. is not the end of the matter. Again, the woman must also show that she "has acted to her detriment or significantly altered her position in reliance on the agreement" before the court will hold that a trust in her favour has arisen.

Two points should be noted concerning this type of trust. First, it can be distinguished from an express trust, which does not require an agreement between the parties, nor the woman having "acted to her detriment". Secondly, it can be distinguished from a trust arising from the common intention of the parties, because the court does not infer an agreement: direct evidence of it must be present.

Obviously, again the crucial issue is the sort of conduct that is required before, for this type of trust, the woman will be held to have acted to her detriment. On this issue, Lord Bridge commented that such conduct could fall:

> "far short of such conduct as would by itself have supported the claim (that a trust had arisen) in the absence of an express representation by the male partner that she was to have ... an interest."

In other words, where there is evidence of an express agreement between the parties, and there is thus no need to persuade the court to draw an inference of common intent from the parties' conduct, the woman need not show direct contributions to the purchase price to prove that she had acted to her detriment in reliance on the agreement. So, what does she have to show?

Lord Bridge cited two cases in which the woman had been held, in his view, correctly, to have a beneficial interest in property vested in the sole name of her male partner: *Grant v Edwards* and *Eves v Eves* (CA 1975). In both, there was evidence of an express agreement that the woman should have a share. In*Grant v Edwards*, the woman had paid the general household bills, as well as for the parties' food. In *Eves v Eves*, the woman had made no financial contribution at all, but had laboured extensively on improvements to the property. In *Grant v Edwards*, the woman's contribution was described variously as:

> "referable to the acquisition of the property" [in the sense that the man could not have afforded to pay the mortgage on the property without the woman paying the other bills, and] "conduct on which the woman could not reasonably have been expected to embark unless she was to have an interest in the house."

In *Eves v Eves*, the woman's contribution was described as "much more than many wives would do".

Comment: This has been an area of law that has seen immense development of principles over the last 45 years. The Lords decisions of *Pettitt v Pettitt* and *Gissing v Gissing* were the first to overtly state the need for the woman to show a common intent; *Grant v Edwards*, the first to overtly state the need for the woman to show that she had acted to her detriment in relying upon it; *Lloyds Bank Plc v Rosset* draws a clear distinction between trusts arising from express discussions and trusts arising from inferences drawn from other types of conduct.

Thus, it is extremely difficult, if not impossible, to synthesise all cases in this area. At best, it involves "reinterpreting" earlier cases in the light of, in particular, the judgment of Lord Bridge in *Lloyds Bank Plc v Rosset* (with which all other Lords agreed).

What is a further matter for concern is Lord Bridge's statement that, where it was necessary for the court to infer a common intent from the conduct of the parties (because there was no evidence of an express agreement), this could only be done from evidence of direct payments to the purchase price.

This particular principle seems extremely difficult to reconcile with earlier authorities. In these, arguably, and with respect to Lord Bridge, some types of indirect financial contributions have been held to be sufficient to raise the inference of common intent and not just been seen as evidence of the woman having acted to her detriment in relying upon express discussions. See, for example, the statements of Lord Diplock in *Gissing v Gissing*, and those of Lords Justices Fox and May in *Burns v Burns* (CA 1984).

Further, if Lord Bridge's statements represent an accurate interpretation of the law, this means that, in cases where the parties do not expressly discuss their intentions as to the ownership of the property, domestic arrangements as to who pays what, possibly made only for the convenience of the parties, will dictate the outcome of an ownership dispute.

From what has been said, it will be appreciated that a woman who has no financial resources of her own to contribute, whether it be directly or indirectly, is at a severe disadvantage.

Lord Bridge's comments two decades or so ago are in stark contrast to the views expressed by the House of Lords in *White v White* (2000) and *McFarlane v McFarlane* where the totally opposite view was taken as to the wife's contribution to the family wealth. But it is important to remember that *Rosset* was decided on the basis of property law, whilst *White* and *McFarlane* were only concerned with s.25 of the **M.C.A.** It should also be noted that neither case overrules or varies the decision in *Rosset*.

Quantification of beneficial interests under a trust

Once it is established that a party does have a beneficial interest it is necessary to quantify the extent of that interest. If the parties declare the shares in which they hold the beneficial interest, that is the end of the matter (*Goodman v Gallant* (1986)). In the case of a resulting trust, the shares are determined in proportion to their financial contribution (*Springette v Defoe* (1992); *Sekhon v Alissa* (1989)). Where there is an implied trust, the shares will be determined by the parties' intentions as determined by the court. This obviously depends on the facts of the particular case and accounts for the inconsistency of the authorities.

However, the Court of Appeal in *Midland Bank v Cooke* (1995) appear to have adopted a new approach which casts doubt on the arithmetic approaches set out above. The court said that once an interest has been established, it may take into account any relevant evidence including indirect contributions such as contributing to household expenses and doing work to the house (which *Rosset* said would not raise the inference of a trust). It could also be inferred from such evidence that the shares should be divided in such proportions as seem equitable at the date of sale, notwithstanding the size of the original contribution.

MIDLAND BANK V COOKE

The couple married in 1971 and the matrimonial home was bought in his sole name. He provided £1,000 towards the deposit and the balance came from a wedding gift of £1,100 from his parents. When she worked, she paid household bills and some contractors' bills. When she ceased work to have children, she did some decorating and other work to the house. It was held at first instance that the wedding gift was a gift to both and thus a direct contribution entitling her to a beneficial interest. The Court of Appeal held on surveying the whole course of dealing between them, including her indirect contributions and the sharing of burdens and advantages, that she would be entitled to a half interest.

The important case is now the House of Lords decision in *Stack v Dowden* [2007].

KEY CASE

STACK V DOWDEN [2007]

Although the house had been conveyed into joint names and there was no declaration of trust, their Lordships were prepared to look at all the circumstances of the case in a domestic consumer situation. The fact that she had provided a greater contribution to the purchase price and that they kept their financial affairs separate meant that she had made out a good case to a claim for 65 per cent of the proceeds.

> "The search is to ascertain the parties' intentions, actual, inferred or imputed ... in the light of their whole course of conduct".
> (Baroness Hale)

KEY CASE

JONES V KERNOTT (2011)

The parties bought the former matrimonial home in joint names but after a long separation, during which she made all the mortgage payments, it was held by the Supreme Court that the property should be held 90 – 10 in her favour by reason of a "common intention" The parties had never had any discussions and the case does not clarify the law any further.

Proprietary estoppel

Estoppel is the principle that prevents a person from exercising or asserting his legal rights and usually the principle can only be pleaded in the defence of an action to exercise or assert those rights. Proprietary estoppel however can also be used to assert contrary rights. Obviously, the circumstances in which such a situation will be recognised by the law are rigorously defined. They have been fully discussed in *Coombes v Smith* (HC 1987), where the court stated that a claim to a share in the beneficial interest of property based upon proprietary estoppel would only succeed if the claimant could show:

(a) that she had made a mistake as to her legal rights in the property;
(b) that she had spent money or done some other act as a result of that mistake;
(c) that the defendant knew of his own rights in the property inconsistent with those she thought she had;
(d) that he knew of her mistaken belief; or
(e) that he encouraged her to act as mentioned above.

(It will be seen that the concept of proprietary estoppel has, of late, heavily influenced the development of the trust principles discussed above.)

The application of the concept can be illustrated by comparing two cases.

COOMBES V SMITH

The relationship had lasted some ten years during which time the plaintiff had borne a child. The home was vested in the sole name of the defendant although the plaintiff had paid for central heating to be installed and for some decorating. Twice the plaintiff had asked for her name to be included on the title deeds and twice the defendant had refused, telling her that she "was not to worry about her future".

Held: the plaintiff had not established that she was entitled to a share in the home on the basis of proprietary estoppel. She had not been mistaken about her rights in the home: on the contrary, she clearly knew that she was not entitled to a share because she had asked for her name to be included on the deeds and he had refused. Even if this conclusion was incorrect, she had not acted relying upon the mistaken belief: her acting as a wife and mother and her paying for decorating and central heating were not behaviour that indicated a reliance upon a mistaken belief as to her rights in the home.

PASCOE V TURNER (CA 1979)

After a relationship of several years had broken down, the man reassured the lady that the house and everything in it were hers. Subsequently, she paid for substantial improvements to the property. The court upheld her claim to a share in the home, even though it was in the sole name of the man, on the basis of proprietary estoppel.

Once it is established that the claimant should be allowed to assert a right to the home contrary to that of the legal owner, the question that must then be answered is the extent of her right. In *Pascoe v Turner* Cumming-Bruce L.J. asked of himself what was "the minimum equity to do justice to her, having regard to the way in which she changed her position for the worse" and decided that the only just solution was that she should be given the whole of the house. Obviously, the relief ordered in any other case will be totally dependent on the facts that have led to the claim.

OCCUPATION OF THE HOME

If a woman is successful in establishing that she has a beneficial interest in the property, she may then be faced with a demand that nevertheless the property be sold so that the man may at least realise his share. This could equally happen to a woman who is a joint owner on the face of the deeds. An immediate sale of the home, on the breakdown of the relationship, can cause just as much hardship to an unmarried woman as it can to a wife, even if she does receive a share of the proceeds of sale.

By s.14 of the Trusts of Land and Appointment of Trustees Act 1996, the court can order the sale of property subject to a trust (as most jointly owned property is). But it can also refuse to make such an order. Generally it will do so if satisfied that the purpose of the trust is still unfulfilled. Thus if the home was in reality bought as a home for the family, it is likely that any application for the sale of the home prior to any children reaching their majority will be refused, despite the fact that the relationship of the adults has broken down. Thus the woman's occupation is protected to a limited extent.

As a last resort, she may be able to show that he granted her a licence to remain in the property. The rules, such as they are based in contract but rely on similar principles to those which apply to implied trusts.

In *Tanner v Tanner* (CA 1975), because the woman gave up a protected tenancy to go and live with the man and their children at his house, the court inferred that he had granted to her a licence to occupy his property until the children left school. However, in *Coombes v Smith* the court rejected the alternative claim of the plaintiff to a licence for the duration of her life. (It was not asked to determine whether the facts led to the inference that she had been granted a licence while the children were of school age because the man had conceded this.)

It will be appreciated that inferring a licence and its terms is an extremely artificial exercise.

REFORM?

The Government asked the Law Commission to look at this whole area and they produced a consultation paper suggesting reforms. Cohabitants could be given similar rights to married couples or civil partners, though cohabitants with children could be given different treatment to those without. The consultation process was completed on September 30, 2006, so it will be some time before possible legislation is forthcoming.

Revision Checklist

By now you should know and understand:

- **the requirement for common intention to establish an interest in property**
- **what evidence may be required to support that intention**
- **the approaches taken by the courts to quantify those interests**

QUESTION AND ANSWER

The Question

Mike (M), a builder, and Winnie (W) a teacher, have never married. When they met four years ago, M had found a house which required renovation but was unable to raise enough money to buy it. W gave him £5,000 to make up the deposit and M signed a document in which he agreed to repay the money within five years. The house was purchased in M's name alone.

Soon afterwards, the parties agreed to set up home together. They talked about their future and agreed that the property should be a "joint effort". W helped with the renovation by labouring at the property. She used her salary to buy food and clothing, to pay for their holidays together and to buy furniture and fittings for the house. Occasionally, she paid some of the mortgage instalments. M used income he saved to renovate the property to a higher standard and, once the work was complete, to take up power boat racing.

Two years ago, W gave birth to their child and stopped work. The relationship deteriorated and M left a week ago. She has now received a letter from M enclosing a cheque for £5,000 in "repayment of the loan" and asking her to leave his house.

Does W have an interest in the house, and if so, to what extent?

Suggested Answer

To establish a trust, W must show either that the parties expressly agreed that they were both beneficially entitled or that an inference that they both intended this can be drawn from their conduct. In either case, W must show that she acted to her detriment in reliance on the agreement or the common intent (*Lloyds Bank v Rosset*). The agreement on "a joint effort" should be enough (*Eves*, *Grant v Edwards*).

Pettitt, *Gissing and Rosset* all require direct contributions to either the purchase price or the mortgage payments. Contributions to food, clothing, holidays, etc. will not do.

But, W has paid to the deposit and mortgage instalments: once this is established *Midland Bank v Cooke* holds that the court can look at the history of the relationship to decide quantum. Using that case, W may very well get a half share.

FINANCIAL PROVISION FOR CHILDREN

4

INTRODUCTION

When the Child Support Act 1991 was introduced in April 1993, it proved to be controversial and unpopular. The situation was exacerbated as the Child Support Agency (the Agency) created to administer the scheme seemed incapable of efficiently or accurately carrying out its business.

To some extent, this was caused by an incredibly complicated formula for calculating maintenance payments but matters did not improve when the calculation was simplified. Reform became a necessity: the new arrangements are set out below, but in essence the Agency has a new name and a new role, that of enforcement only.

C.S.A.—a fresh start

Only a minority of cases handled by the Agency actually received any maintenance and over £3 billion of debt was built up.

It was for these reasons that the Government asked Sir David Henshaw to begin a fundamental redesign of our whole system of child support. He presented his recommendations for change in July 2006. The system should be simpler, less bureaucratic and more cost-effective.

Whether or not a person decides to use the state system to arrange child maintenance should be their choice. The system should prioritise the needs of children and help engender a new climate where parents can more easily come to their own financial arrangements. They would no longer be required to apply to the Agency.

The Government accepted the recommendations which led to the Child Maintenance and Other Payments Act 2008. The Act has added a variety of new enforcement provisions to the child support scheme by amendment of the existing C.S.A. 1991. The powers derived from the 2008 Act will be added to the existing provisions and will be operated by the Child Support Maintenance Commission (the "Commission") replacing the Agency. Under the scheme set up by the 2008 Act ss.20–30, various new forms of enforcement are introduced; and the liability order (now under s.32M) becomes an administrative direction. The new provisions will then be introduced alongside the existing forms of enforcement under C.S.A. 1991 ss.35–40. In addition to the recast liability order the new enforcement provisions comprise: power to deduct continuing payments of child maintenance or arrears direct from a person's bank or other account; a specific form of freezing order, obtainable in the High Court; powers for the magistrates to impose a curfew and removal of passports alongside the existing committal and disqualification orders; and the power to recover from the estate of a dead liable parent.

A new "liability order" emerges under s.32M described by the 2008 Act s.25 as an "administrative liability order". The same liability "order" can therefore now be deployed by the Commission to seek the original remedies introduced by the **C.S.A.**—distress, county court order and committal—as well as being used to obtain the new: passport control and curfew orders under the 2008 Act.

The C.S.A. regime

The **C.S.A.** introduced a hugely complicated formula for calculating child maintenance but this was reformed by the **Child Support, Pensions and Social Security Act 2000** (**C.S.P.S.S.A.**) The "non-resident parent" pays 15 per cent of his net assessable income for one child, 20 per cent for two and 25 per cent for three or more, with a ceiling of £2000 per week. His net income can be reduced by similar percentages where he has children who reside with him, for example, step-children.

Liability is imposed on the child's natural parents but only where one or both are living in the same household as the child.

Where the alleged father denies paternity, s.27 of the **C.S.A.** 1991 provides that the Secretary of State or the carer of the child may apply to the court (i.e. High Court, County Court or Family Proceedings Court) for a declaration of parentage. This means that it is then open to the court to direct that D.N.A. testing be carried out to determine the issue. The putative father has a right of appeal against any maintenance assessment which may be made against him.

Where the carer parent is in receipt of income support, family credit, or disability working allowance she is required to authorise the Secretary of State to take action to recover child support maintenance from the absent parent (s.6).

Where the carer parent refuses to authorise the Agency to seek maintenance or to provide them with information to assess the maintenance liability of the non-resident parent, that parent's benefit may be reduced (s.46).

If the officer of the Agency considers that there are reasonable grounds for believing that the claimant or child would suffer harm or undue distress, no further action will be taken. This is an area of the Act where the officer has considerable discretion, but, in exercising his discretion, he is required to have regard to the welfare of any child likely to be affected by his decision. However, where no reasonable grounds are established, the benefit (whether income support or family credit) will be reduced by 20 per cent for 26 weeks and 10 per cent for a further 52 weeks.

Where the carer is not in receipt of family credit or income support, there is a choice so far as claiming maintenance for the child is concerned:

(a) apply to the Agency for a maintenance assessment; or
(b) enter into a maintenance agreement with the non-resident parent.

However, the parent with care cannot be prevented from seeking a maintenance assessment even where an agreement or court has been made. Any attempt to restrict the right to apply for such an assessment is void (s.9(4)).

Since April 1995 recognition has been given of the need to take account of the position of the non-resident parent who had transferred capital, usually in the form of the matrimonial home, to the parent with care. This has been achieved by giving the non-resident parent a further allowance calculated rateably according to the value of the property transferred.

The **C.S.P.S.S.A.** amended previous legislation by introducing "Variations" intended for use in "clearly exceptional cases".

The overall effect will be to permit the Agency to take account of certain circumstances, such as additional expenses borne by the absent parent, the fact that the absent parent has transferred property to the parent with care or that the parent with care is not utilising an asset to maximise its income producing potential so as to reduce the maintenance assessment which would otherwise be payable.

The additional expenses include:

(a) costs incurred in long distance travelling to work;
(b) costs incurred by an absent parent in maintaining contact with the child (for example, travel expenses);
(c) debts incurred before the parent became an absent parent in relation to the child. Though "debts" are not defined, certain debts are excluded, including gambling debts, trade or business debts and use of credit cards; and
(d) pre-1993 commitments which it is impossible or would be unreasonable to expect the parent concerned to withdraw from.

Each are subject to rigorous conditions before it can qualify for consideration and even then, the Secretary of State must form the opinion that it would be just and equitable to grant them.

In recognition that having contact involves financial cost, the non-resident parent can reduce payments when the child stays overnight. The amounts start at one seventh for 52 nights rising to one half for 175 nights.

Orders for children under the Matrimonial Causes Act 1973

Although the **C.S.A.** supplants the court's powers, the sections of the **M.C.A.** and **C.A.** dealing with child maintenance are not repealed and it is still necessary to discuss these provisions. The courts will have a role in any of the following circumstances:

(i) Where the absent parent is sufficiently wealthy to be able to "top up" the maximum maintenance which can be assessed under **C.S.A**.

(ii) Where the child is receiving full-time instruction or training requiring provision of some or all of the expenses, e.g. school fees.

(iii) Where the child is disabled, orders may be made to meet some or all of the expenses attributable to that disability.

(iv) Where 17 and 18-year-olds are not in full-time education.

(v) Where there is to be a lump sum or transfer of property order.

(vi) Where the child is a "child of the family" and not a qualifying child under the **C.S.A**.

Within the limitations of the above conditions children can have the same types of orders made in their favour, against either of the parties to the marriage or the civil partnership as can the parties themselves.

The order can direct payment to the child or some third party for the child's benefit. Obviously, the "third party" will usually be the parent who has the child living with him.

Generally, no application for an order in favour of a child over 18 can be made. The orders can be made on the grant of a decree or at any time afterwards, but it should be noted that in the case of periodical payments, secured and unsecured, and lump sum the order can also be made before the grant of a decree or, if the proceedings for decree are unsuccessful, on the dismissal of the petition or within a reasonable time afterwards. Thus, to a certain extent, children can be provided for independently of a decree.

Periodical payments orders secured or unsecured must terminate when the child reaches 17, unless the court considers that the welfare of the child requires the order to extend beyond that age. Further, neither order can extend beyond 18 unless the court is satisfied that the child is still (or would be) receiving education or training for employment or there are other special circumstances. Finally, both types of periodical payments orders must cease on the death of the payer, even secured payments.

Matters taken into account when making orders As with spouse orders, the first consideration of the court, when deciding whether and how to exercise its powers, is the welfare of any minor children of the family.

The courts are provided with a list of matters that they must have regard to by s.25(3) of the **M.C.A.**:

(a) the financial needs of the child;

(b) the income, earning capacity, property and other financial resources of the child;

(c) any physical or mental disability of the child;

(d) the type of education or training he was receiving or was expected to receive by the parties to the marriage; and

(e) the financial assets and needs of the parties, the standard of living enjoyed by the family prior to the breakdown of the marriage, and any physical or mental disability of the parties.

Section 25(4) of the **M.C.A.** provides further factors to be taken into account when the court is considering making an order against a party to the marriage who is not a parent of the child, and include, for example, the liability of any other person to maintain the child.

Orders under s.15 of the Children Act 1989

Section 15 of the **C.A.** provides for the grant of a range of financial and property awards for the benefit of a child. The applicant must be the parent (or guardian) of the child and orders can be made against a parent.

It must be remembered that the availability of these orders is not dependent upon the parties being married to each other; it is dependent upon parenthood. However, married parents may make use of s.15 where there is no pending divorce proceedings.

Once parenthood has been established, the court has the power to make the following orders:

(a) that either parent pay periodical payments for the benefit of the child, secured or unsecured;

(b) that either parent pay a lump sum for the benefit of the child;

(c) that either parent transfer property to which he is entitled to the child; and

(d) that either parent do settle such property for the benefit of the child.

Payments and transfer for the benefit of the child can be ordered to be made direct to the child himself or to some third party. (It should be noted that if the application is made to a magistrates' court, the only orders that can be made are ones for unsecured periodical payments and lump sums not exceeding £1,000.)

All the above orders benefit children alone. Subject to this limitation, the range of orders available under s.15 of the **C.A.** is wide, almost equivalent to those available ancillary to decree proceedings.

Orders for unsecured periodical payments cease on the death of the payer and for both types of periodical payment the rules for cessation when the child reaches a specified age, covered in Ch.2 in connection with the **M.C.A.**, apply.

Schedule 1 to the C.A. lists the matters that the court must take into account when deciding what order to make. They bear some similarity to those listed in s.25(3) of the **M.C.A.** especially the factors relevant for child orders ancillary to decree proceedings.

Revision Checklist

By now you should know and understand:

- **the main provisions of the C.S.A. and how it has been reformed**

- **the alternative claims which may be brought under the M.C.A and the C.A.**

QUESTION AND ANSWER

The Question

Discuss and explain the range and scope of the statutory provisions for child maintenance

Suggested Answer

You should be prepared to address three main areas: the **C.S.A.**, the **M.C.A.** and the **C.A.**

The **C.S.A.** is a failed regime but until its final demise its main provisions should be referred to. The original complex formula has been replaced by a simpler percentage of earnings (which you will not be expected to elaborate on) but the compulsory referrals by parents on benefit included draconian measures of disclosure of the absent parents details and limited variations for the payer to take into account living expenses and other dependants. Reductions could also be made where there is contact with the child. Under the 2008 Act, when fully implemented, the emphasis will be on parents reaching agreement but the Commission replacing the Agency with have extended powers to enforce payment.

The **M.C.A.** provides for maintenance for children who did not fall under the **C.S.A.** or whose needs were not met by that regime. The matters taken into account are similar to the specified matters in s.25. The orders are similar as well but can only be made as part of divorce etc. proceedings.

Section 15 of the **C.A.** is available as a free standing application to any parent to claim financial provision for a child against the other parent, irrespective of their marital status. The range of orders is similar to that available in ancillary relief proceedings.

DOMESTIC VIOLENCE

INTRODUCTION

Violence in the family is not unknown. It can occur in many forms including behaviour which falls short of violence in the accepted sense of the word. It may cause the breakdown of a relationship or arise from it: the victim may not even accept that the relationship is ended.

It should be remembered that physical violence wherever and with whomever committed is a criminal offence. In the landmark decision of *R. v R.* (1992) the House of Lords ruled that a husband can rape his wife, overturning the medieval common law. However, the criminal law is primarily concerned with punishment and does not always adequately protect the victim. Therefore this chapter is concerned with civil remedies of which the most effective is the injunction, in particular;

1. Non-molestation orders under the F.L.A. 1996;
2. Occupation orders under the same Act;
3. Injunctions under the Protection from Harassment Act 1997.

An injunction can be granted not only to restrain violence but also to restrain "molestation". For the sake of brevity, the term violence will be used in this chapter but will include, unless otherwise stated, molestation as well.

KEY CASE

Horner v Horner (CA 1983) defined molestation as "any conduct which can properly be regarded as such a degree of harassment as to call for the intervention of the Court".

There are cases where an injunction restraining such behaviour will not be sufficient protection. Families living under the same roof while a relationship is breaking down are subject to all sorts of pressures which cannot always be solved by non-molestation orders. Sometimes, they simply add to the pressures.

In these cases, there may be no real alternative but to make an order separating the parties, an order which removes a partner from the home and regulates the occupation of it.

It is most commonly the woman who seeks an order against the man and this assumption is used throughout the chapter. The powers can be equally used by a man against a woman. It should also be noted that orders can be granted for the protection of children in the family.

PART IV OF THE FAMILY LAW ACT 1996

Part IV was implemented on October 1, 1997 and repealed a "hotchpot of legislation" and an unsatisfactory state of affairs.

Associated persons

The **F.L.A.** gives remedies to a much wider range of people than the legislation it replaced. There is now a list of "Associated Persons" who may apply for injunctions. A person is associated with another person if:

(a) They are or have been married to each other or are, or have been, civil partners.

(b) They are cohabitants or former cohabitants; "cohabitants" are a man and a woman who, although not married to each other, are living together as husband and wife. "Former cohabitants" is to be read accordingly but does not include co-habitants who have subsequently married each other.

(c) They live or have lived in the same household, otherwise merely by reason of one of them being the other's employee, tenant, lodger or boarder. This will probably cover those in a same-sex relationship.

(d) They are relatives.

(e) They have agreed to marry one another (whether or not that agreement has been terminated). There has to be evidence of the agreement such as a ring or a ceremony.

(f) In relation to any child they are either the parent of the child or a person who has or has had parental responsibility for the child.

(g) They are parties to the same family proceedings.

Not only may they make their own application but they may include in the order a "Relevant Child", that is:

(a) any child who is living with or might reasonably be expected to live with either of the parties;

(b) any child in relation to whom an order under the Adoption Act 1976 or the C.A. is in question in the proceedings; or

(c) any other child whose interests the court considers relevant.

Children under 16 can apply for an order with leave and if of sufficient understanding. Under **C.A.** amendments a parent may be removed from the home instead of taking a child into Local Authority care.

NON-MOLESTATION ORDERS

Section 42 of the **F.L.A.** allows the court to make orders prohibiting a person from molesting a person with whom he is associated and from molesting a relevant child.

The order may refer to molestation in general or particular acts of molestation or both, and may be made for a specified period or until further order. In exercising its discretion the court shall have to regard all the circumstances including the need to secure the health, safety and well being of the applicant or of any relevant child.

There is no definition of molestation in the **F.L.A.** so all the existing case law remains relevant. For example, injunctions were granted in the following cases:

> **HORNER V HORNER (CA 1983)**
> The husband hung scurrilous posters about his wife on the railings of the school where she worked.

> **SPENCER V CAMACHO (1983)**
> Inter alia, he searched through her handbag without her permission.

> **JOHNSON V WALTON (1990)**
> He sent nude photographs of his former lover to the newspapers.

OCCUPATION ORDERS

These orders were introduced by the **F.L.A.** and are available to "associated persons". The terms and duration of the order will depend upon the parties entitlement to occupy the property. It is suggested that the best approach is to deal with the different orders on the basis of the different scenarios which can arise under the **F.L.A.**

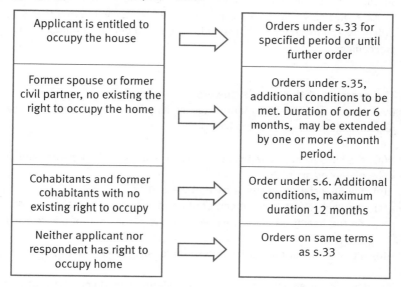

Although the **F.L.A.** was drafted to comply with the **Human Rights Act** there is potential for conflict in that art.8 gives everyone the right to respect for his private and family life and his home. Equally, these measures may be justified on the grounds of protection of others.

The applicant is entitled to occupy the property

Section 33 of the **F.L.A.** is likely to be the most common ground for such orders because the basis is that an application can be made by any person who is entitled to occupy a dwelling-house by virtue of a beneficial estate or interest or contract or has matrimonial home rights in relation to that house. It must be or must have been the home of the person entitled and of another person with whom she is associated or was at any time intended by them to be their home.

An order under s.33 may:

(a) enforce the applicants entitlement to enter and or remain in occupation of the house or even part of it;

(b) prohibit, suspend or restrict the exercise by the respondent of any right of his to occupy the house, including his matrimonial home rights; and

(c) regulate the occupation of the dwelling-house by either or both parties.

Unlike earlier legislation where orders were limited to three-month periods of time, an order can be made for a specified period, until the occurrence of a

specified event or until further order. It should be remembered that under the
F.L.A., a divorce would have taken a minimum of 12 months so that s.33
Orders may be related to such a period when issued prior to or during divorce
proceedings.

The exercise of the court's powers

By s.33(6), in deciding whether to exercise its powers, the court shall have
regard to all the circumstances including:

(a)   the housing needs and housing resources of each of the parties and of
      any relevant child;
(b)   the financial resources of each of the parties;
(c)   the likely effect of any order, or of any decision not to make an order,
      on the health, safety or well being of the parties and of any relevant
      child; and
(d)   the conduct of the parties in relation to each other and otherwise.

These provisions are similar to those in the Matrimonial Homes Act 1967 and
cases decided under that Act may give useful guidance to the new
provisions.

> #### RICHARDS V RICHARDS (1972)
> Her divorce petition catalogued a number of minor complaints,
> described as "flimsy in the extreme". She sought an "Ouster Order"
> because she could not bear to be in the same house with him. The trial
> judge made the order on the grounds that he had to put the children
> first. The House of Lords revoked the order; all factors carried equal
> weight and his conduct did not justify the making of such an order.

> #### WISEMAN V SIMPSON (1988)
> There was no history of violence but the atmosphere in the home was
> tense. Eventually, she changed the locks while he was out and denied
> him entry. The court held that this was "a serious wrong" which the
> court would not allow her to take advantage of.

The balance of harm test

The court has complete discretion to make an order except under s.33(7) of
the **F.L.A.** If it appears to the court that the applicant or any relevant child is
likely to suffer significant harm, attributable to conduct of the respondent if
an order is not made, the court shall make the order (i.e. is under a duty to do
so) unless it appears to it that the respondent or any relevant child is likely to

suffer significant harm if the order is made and that harm is as great, or greater than the harm which is likely to be suffered by the applicant or child if the order is not made.

Applicant is a former spouse, a former civil partner, a cohabitant or a former cohabitant with no existing right to occupy

Section 35 of the **F.L.A.** applies if a former spouse or civil partner is entitled to occupy a dwelling house by virtue of a beneficial estate, etc. and the other former spouse or civil partner is not so entitled; and the house was at any time their matrimonial home or was at any time intended by them to be their matrimonial home. For the purposes of this section, a person claiming an equitable interest in the home is deemed not to have a right to occupy.

Sections 36 and 37 of the **F.L.A.** make similar provision for cohabitants and ex-cohabitants who also do not have rights to occupy the former family home. Where the applicant is a former spouse, the court shall have regard not only to the matters set out in s.33(6) (see above) but also:

(a) the length of time that has elapsed since the parties ceased to live together;

(b) the length of time that has elapsed since the marriage was dissolved or annulled; and

(c) the existence of any pending proceedings between the parties for property adjustment orders under ss.23A or 24 of the **M.C.A.**, or orders for financial relief under the C.A. or relating to the ownership of the dwelling house.

Where the applicant is a cohabitant or ex-cohabitant with no entitlement to occupy, additional circumstances to be taken into account are:

(i) the nature of the parties' relationship;

(ii) the length of time during which they have lived together as husband and wife; and

(iii) whether there are or have been any children who are children of both parties or for whom they have or have had parental responsibility.

The terms of the orders are the same as those available under s.33 of the **F.L.A.** (see above) but the duration of the orders will differ.

An order in respect of former spouses or civil partners:

(a) may not be made after the death of either of the former spouses;

(b) ceases to have effect on the death of either of them; and

(c) must be limited so as to have effect for a specified period not exceeding six months, but may be extended on one or more occasions for a further specified period not exceeding six months.

In respect of cohabitants and former cohabitants, an order may not exceed six months and may be extended on only one occasion for a further six months, i.e. a maximum of 12 months. Further, the "Balance of Harm" provisions require the court merely "to have regard" to the possible harm. In other words, the court retains a discretion as opposed to the duty imposed in other sections.

Applicant is a spouse, a former spouse, a civil partner or former civil partner, a cohabitant or a former cohabitant and neither applicant nor respondent has a right to occupy

Sections 37 and 38 of the **F.L.A.** deal with these situations, which are likely to be rare in practice. They deal with persons who occupy their homes under contracts with their employers or live in homes owned by their parents, for example. Whatever their circumstances, the court is empowered to make orders in the same terms as under s.33 of the **F.L.A.**

Additional powers

By virtue of s.40 of the **F.L.A.** the court may on making an occupation order, or at any time after:

(a) impose on either party obligations as to repair and maintenance of the house or the discharge of rent, mortgage or other outgoings;
(b) order a party occupying the house or any part of it to make periodical payments to the other in respect of the accommodation;
(c) grant either party possession or use of furniture or other contents, subject to taking reasonable care of the same; or
(d) order either party to take reasonable steps to keep the house and any furniture or other contents secure.

In deciding whether, and if so, how to exercise its power the court shall have regard to all the circumstances of the case including the financial needs and resources of the parties and the financial obligations which they have or are likely to have including financial obligations to each other and to any relevant child.

Applications for non-molestation orders or occupation orders can be made ancillary to other family proceedings or as free standing applications in their own right (ss.42(2)(a) and 39(2) of the **F.L.A.**).

PROTECTION FROM HARASSMENT ACT 1997

This Act came into force on June 18, 1997. Although it is intended as a remedy against "stalking", it is sufficiently wide to cover domestic situations as well. Section 1 provides that a person must not pursue a course of conduct which amounts to harassment of another and which he knows or ought to know amounts to harassment. The test is: would a reasonable person possessing the same information think the conduct amounted to harassment?

Section 2 creates a summary offence and s.4 an indictable offence where a person is put in fear of violence. The courts are empowered, in addition to any other punishment, to issue restraining orders forbidding the offender from doing anything specified by the order for the purpose of protecting the victim. Further, s.3 creates a statutory tort of harassment and provides for the issue of injunctions, the breach of which entitles the plaintiff to apply for a warrant to arrest the defendant.

ENFORCEMENT

It is one thing to obtain an injunction or order designed to protect family members and quite another to ensure that it is obeyed. In many cases, such orders are broken and the topic of how to enforce obedience to such orders is, in practice, very important.

It is obvious that no court can directly force respondents to comply with such orders. Applicants must rely on the court's powers to punish respondents for disobedience and hope that this (or the threat of it) will, indirectly, force respondents to obey such orders in the future. Breach of an injunction granted by either the High Court or the County Court is contempt and is punishable by either a fine or, more usually in this context, imprisonment.

To obtain the punishment of the respondent by either of these methods, the applicant must take the responsibility for the institution and continuation of the process, a factor that can cause great stress and anxiety for a person who has already undergone much. She will often seek the help of her solicitor at all stages of the process, thus increasing the costs, and the process takes time. To avoid some, if not all of these disadvantages, a power of arrest can be attached to injunctions and orders. The effect of this, is that a police constable can arrest, without warrant, any person whom he reasonably suspects of having broken the order. The only initiative the applicant must take is to contact the police immediately upon breach—far better than having to wait until her solicitor's office and the court office open—and they can take him into custody immediately. The police must bring such a person before the relevant court within 24 hours, and the court can then punish by fine or imprisonment.

The exercise of a power of arrest has immediate and dire consequences for the alleged offender. Consequently, its grant is hedged about by limitations.

The **Domestic Violence, Crime and Victims Act 2004** makes it a criminal offence to flout civil orders relating to non-molestation even where a power of arrest has not been attached. It also makes common assault an arrestable offence and aims to improve liaison between criminal and civil courts. There is an emphasis on victim support.

Revision Checklist

By now you should know and understand:

- who are "associated persons" for the purposes of the **F.L.A.** Part IV

- the orders available and conditions to be satisfied

- the scope of the Protection from Harassment Act

QUESTION AND ANSWER

The Question

(i) Jane is married to Charles and the matrimonial home is in his name alone. Charles threatened physical violence to Jane and their two young children, so Jane fled the house with them. She has nowhere to live and wishes to return to the matrimonial home, but not to Charles.

(ii) Gillian wants to eject her lover Michael from their home as he has recently attacked her three times following excessive drinking sessions. The house is in his sole name.

(iii) Trevor once went on a date with Rachel. Since then, she has pestered him with phone calls and has now begun waiting outside his workplace and his parents' house (where he lives) hoping to catch a glimpse of him.

Advise Jane, Gillian and Trevor as to the remedies available to them.

Suggested Answer

(i) Jane and Charles are associated persons for the purposes of Pt IV of the **F.L.A.**

J will have matrimonial home rights and is a person entitled to occupy for the purposes of s.33. She can apply for an occupation order, taking into account the matters set out in s.33(6) including conduct, housing needs, financial resources and safety and well being of the parties including the children.

Section 33(7) requires the court to apply the "balance of harm" test and must make an order if J and the children are likely to suffer greater harm than C if an order is not made.

The order can be for a specified period or until further order.

J could also seek a non-molestation order under s.42.

(ii) Gillian and Michael are also associated persons but as a cohabitant, she has no matrimonial home rights. She will apply under s.36. Similar criteria but the court must additionally consider the nature of the parties' relationship and the length of time they have lived together.

The "balance of harm" is taken into account but no duty is imposed on the court.

The duration of the order is six months renewable for one further period of six months.

G may also apply for a non-molestation order.

(iii) Trevor and Rachel are not associated persons so no remedy is available under **F.L.A.**

If a reasonable person would believe that R's conduct amounts to harassment, she will have committed an offence under s.1 of the **Protection from Harassment Act 1997**. The court can impose a restraining order in addition to any other punishment.

R also commits the statutory tort of harassment entitling T to injunctive relief.

THE RELATIONSHIP BETWEEN CHILDREN AND ADULTS

6

INTRODUCTION

All references to section numbers within this chapter are references to sections in the **Children Act 1989**, unless otherwise stated.

At birth, the law defines a relationship between a child and his parents and no other adults. For many children, the law plays no further part in their upbringing, but, for some, events subsequent to their birth result in the need for additional principles. Parents may disagree about the child's upbringing; other adults may be the most appropriate carers. This chapter, therefore, covers:

1. The question of who is the parent;
2. The relationship between children and adults, not necessarily their parents, and also the principles the courts use when required to intervene and in some sense redraw the relationship created at birth.

WHO IS THE PARENT?

Medical advances in human assisted reproduction have caused problems which resulted in the passing of Human Fertilisation and Embryology Act 1990, which took effect on August 1, 1991 but relates only to births after that date. That Act has since been superseded by the Human Fertilisation and Embryology Act 2008 but for the purposes of this discussion, little has changed.

There are various types of assisted reproduction, including artificial insemination, in vitro fertilisation (in lay terms, "test-tube" babies) but as either the sperm or the embryo (or both) may be donated by strangers, it means that a child may not be genetically related to its "parents". Section 33(1) of the 2008 Act provides "The woman who is carrying or has carried a child as a result of the placing in her of an embryo or of sperm and eggs, and no other woman, is to be treated as the mother of the child".

As far as the male is concerned, the rule is that the genetic father (i.e. the donor of the sperm) is the legal father. However, there are two important exceptions to this rule. First, by s.35 "Where a married woman is carrying a child ... notwithstanding that the sperm was not donated by the husband, he and no other person is treated as the father of the child". This section will only apply if the husband consented to the wife's treatment. Secondly, by s.36 if donated sperm is used in the course of "licensed treatment" (i.e. licensed under the 2008 Act) for a woman and a man who satisfies "fatherhood conditions" then that man is treated as the father of the child. Basically this means that the man and woman give written notice to "the responsible person" that they consent to treatment and wish him to be treated as the father.

The 2008 Act also deals with surrogacy, where another woman (the surrogate mother) carries the child for a married couple following fertilisation using the gametes of one or both of the applicants. It should be noted that the Act does not apply where the surrogate is impregnated by sexual inter-course with the husband.

Figure 8: Conditions to be met for making a parental order

Under s.54, the court is empowered to make an order (a "Parental Order") that the child is to be treated as a child of the applicants, but the following conditions must be satisfied:

(a) the child has been carried by a woman who is not one of the applicants, as a result of the placing in her of an embryo or sperm and eggs or her artificial insemination;

(b) the gametes of at least one of the applicants were used to bring about the creation of the embryo; and

(c) The applicants must be—
   (i)   husband and wife,
   (ii) civil partners of each other, or
   (iii) two persons who are living as partners in an enduring family relationship and are not within prohibited degrees of relationship in relation to each other.
   (iv) The order must be within six months of the birth.
   (v)   The court must be satisfied that the surrogate mother and the genetic father fully understand and consent to the order.
   (vi) The child's home must be with the applicants.
   (vii) The court must also be satisfied that no money or benefits changed hands in connection with the arrangements (commercial surrogacy is a criminal offence).

PATERNITY DISPUTES

Motherhood is rarely an issue; fatherhood often is, and whenever it falls to be considered, unless paternity is admitted, it must be proved.

Such an issue could arise within a number of different types of proceedings and the courts will often need to determine the paternity of the child as a preliminary matter. For example, only a father is entitled to apply for an order under s.4 (see later). If a man makes such an application, the mother may first deny that the child is his. If she were correct, then the court would not have jurisdiction to grant the order sought. Therefore, faced with such a case, the court would first have to determine whether or not the child was the applicant's.

The question of paternity can also be dealt with as an issue in its own right. Under the **Family Law Act 1986**, a person can apply to the court simply for a declaration that a named person is his father.

Paternity disputes can arise between spouses but they more frequently arise between unmarried partners, possibly due to the following evidentiary point. Any children born to a married woman are presumed to be those of her husband. This presumption is rebuttable but this is not an easy task. There is no similar presumption to come to the aid of the unmarried man or woman who is asserting paternity, even if their relationship is stable and longstanding.

Paternity can be established in a number of different ways: for example, evidence may be adduced of out of court admissions made by the man; of the fact that the man is registered as the father in the Register of Births, Deaths and Marriages; of the man having had sexual intercourse with the mother at the time that conception must have taken place. None of these are conclusive and may or may not be accepted in any given case.

Conclusions drawn from the results of blood tests have also frequently been given as evidence in paternity cases. Until recently, the method of testing could not provide conclusive proof of paternity, but the advent of "D.N.A. fingerprinting" has dramatically altered the position. This can be used on any type of human tissue, for example, blood, hair, skin and semen, and can provide virtually conclusive proof of paternity. Despite the cost of the tests and the limited testing facilities, evidence gained by testing blood by D.N.A. fingerprinting is being used in paternity disputes more frequently.

D.N.A. fingerprinting is only of use if all parties, the mother, the child and the alleged father are tested. The Family Law Reform Act 1969 (F.L.R.A.) provides that, where the parentage of any person is in issue, the court may order that person or a party to the proceedings submit to blood tests. An amendment to the Act effected by the F.L.R.A. gives the court power to order the taking of any bodily samples. If anyone refuses to comply with the order, then the court may draw such inferences from this refusal as it thinks fit. In a case prior to the implementation of the Human Rights Act, the CA thought that the F.L.R.A. was incompatible with the former Act.

STATUS OF CHILDREN

The legal effect of the physical relationship between parent and child is sometimes dependent upon whether the child was born to married or unmarried parents. The phrase "a child whose mother and father were married at the time of his birth" is defined in s.1 of the F.L.R.A. and does include various children who were not literally born to parents who were married at the time of their births, for example, those who are legitimated by the subsequent marriage of their parents. In this book, the phrase "a child born to married parents" includes all those who are covered by the definition in s.1 and the phrase "a child born to unmarried parents" includes all those who are not.

At common law, a child born to unmarried parents had no rights against his father and remoter ancestors and, to begin with, no rights even against his mother: similarly, the adults had no duties towards him. Gradually, with changes in the law the disadvantages have now all but been eradicated.

One of the remaining distinctions drawn by the law between the two categories of children concerns the vesting of parental responsibility in their parents (see below).

PARENTAL RESPONSIBILITY

What is parental responsibility?

This concept is the legal definition of the relationship between parent and child (although sometimes, as will be seen, it also defines the relationship between other adults and a child). It is a new concept introduced by the **C.A.** An appreciation of its nature, as discussed in the whole of this section, is of vital importance: the law relating to the resolution of disputes between private individuals (see Ch.7) and the law relating to the protection of children by local authority intervention (see Ch.8) are built upon it. During the passage through Parliament of the Children Bill, the concept of parental responsibility was aptly described by the Lord Chancellor as:

> "a golden thread, knotting together parental status and the effect of orders about the child's upbringing, whether in private family proceedings or in care proceedings ..."

Previously, the parent/child relationship was thought, very loosely, to be one of parental rights, but in the last few decades this interpretation was criticised and gradually redefined.

KEY CASE

In *Gillick v West Norfolk Area Health Authority and D.H.S.S.* (HL 1985) Lord Scarman stated that:

> "Parental rights are derived from parental duty and exist only so long as they are needed for the protection of the person and property of the child."

This view of parental duty being the key to the definition of the relationship between parent and child has received statutory acknowledgement in the C.A.

> Parental responsibility is defined by s.3 as: "all the rights, duties, powers, responsibilities and authority which by law a parent of a child has in relation to the child and his property."

As will be appreciated, this definition is very general and does not list the sort of issues that are the subject of parental responsibility. Drawing upon cases prior to **C.A.** it is suggested that the concept includes the responsibilities:

(a) to have possession of the child and to take, on his behalf, all the many and minor decisions that arise every day;

(b) to maintain contact with the child (obviously, only applicable if the child does not live with the parent);

(c) to actively consider and provide for the child's education;

(d) to actively consider the need and provide for medical treatment on the child's behalf;

(e) to administer the child's property;

(f) to actively consider the wisdom of and consent or otherwise to the child's marriage between the ages of 16 and 18;

(g) to protect the child from physical and moral danger; and

(h) to maintain the child financially.

To whom does parental responsibility belong?

At the birth of a child, the position is as follows: the parental responsibility for a child born to married parents belongs to both parents (s.2(1)); the parental responsibility for a child born to unmarried parents belongs exclusively to the mother (s.2(2)).

The Law Commission, in its Review of Child Law, Guardianship and Custody No.172, recommended against the automatic creation of equal responsibility for unmarried parents. It was recognised that, while some children are born within stable unions, others are born as a result of a very casual relationship and it was not thought appropriate to give automatic parental responsibility to a man who, in practice, may have nothing to do with the child.

However, the Law Commission did feel that some provision for a sharing of parental responsibility between unmarried parents should be made. Accordingly, s.4 (as amended) provides methods whereby parental responsibility can be given to the unmarried father and thereafter shared with the mother or civil partner.

Figure 9: Who has Parental responsibility?

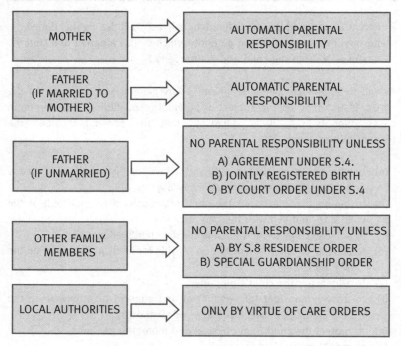

First, it is possible for the parents to agree to share parental responsibility. The agreement, "a Parental Responsibility Agreement" must be in writing, in a prescribed form and recorded in the Principal Registry of the Family Division. In the alternative, the father may apply to the court, who can order that he shall share the parental responsibility for the child with the mother.

On making an application under s.4, the court considers the degree of commitment which the father has shown the child, the attachment which exists between them and the reasons for his application; *Re H (Local Authority: Parental Rights)* (1991). The welfare principle also applies.

It should be noted that the s.4 order merely gives the father status and no more: questions concerning residence and contact are determined by s.8 orders.

Orders or agreements are not permanent; either can be revoked by an order of the court: *Re P (terminating parental responsibility)* (1995).

The number of registered s.4 agreements has been relatively small, probably because lay people are unaware of them.

Under the Adoption and Children Act 2002 (**A.C.A.**) an unmarried father now obtains parental responsibility if he registers the child's birth jointly with the mother.

Parental responsibility, or a large part of it, can be obtained by persons other than the parents of the child. There are several possibilities. There are a number of court orders which have the effect of vesting parental responsibility in the person awarded the order, e.g. a residence order under s.8 and its proposed replacement the **Child Arrangements Order** (see Ch.7) or an adoption or care order (see Ch.8). Section 115 of the **A.C.A.** creates a new concept of "Special Guardian" who will obtain parental responsibility by court order (see Ch.9). Again, the Act gives step-parents the opportunity to acquire parental responsibility in manner similar to provisions made in s.4 of the **C.A.** for unmarried fathers. Finally, a parent with parental responsibility may appoint a guardian for his child and such an appointment will vest parental responsibility in the guardian on the death of that parent (s.5).

The termination of parental responsibility

Apart from the appointment of a guardian or an agreement between unmarried parents, it is impossible for a person with parental responsibility to voluntarily surrender or transfer the whole or any part of it to another (s.2(9)). The exercise of it may be delegated to a third party however.

Parental responsibility is not lost as a result of some other person subsequently acquiring it (s.2(6)).

Subject to what is said below, parental responsibility can only be terminated by court order and only where this is specifically provided for.

For parents married when their child was born and an unmarried mother, parental responsibility can only be terminated by the grant of an adoption order in favour of someone else. Adoption also has this effect on others who have acquired parental responsibility. Further, their parental responsibility can be terminated by an order revoking or discharging the instrument, agreement or order that gave them parental responsibility.

Parental responsibility is owed to a child, defined in the **C.A.** as a person under the age of 18 (save for certain aspects of financial responsibility). Thus, generally, parental responsibility terminates automatically when the child reaches 18. There is also a possibility that parental responsibility terminates automatically at some earlier though as yet ill defined point, as a result of the decision in *Gillick v West Norfolk Area Health Authority*. It must be emphasised that this is a case that predates the **C.A.**, as the following discussion of it, with its use of the term "parental rights", makes clear.

KEY CASE

GILLICK V WEST NORFOLK AREA HEALTH AUTHORITY (1985)
The Area Health Authority (A.H.A.) had issued to the doctors practising in its area a directive which contained guidelines as to when, in the

view of the A.H.A., it would be lawful for a doctor to give contraceptive advice and treatment to a child under the age of 16, without the consent or even knowledge of the child's parent. The plaintiff sought a declaration that the directive was unlawful and one of her arguments was that such advice or treatment was an infringement of parental rights.

The majority of the Lords did not think that this was inevitably so. Lord Scarman stated, inter alia, that "parental rights yield to the right of the child to make his own decision when he reaches a sufficient understanding and intelligence to be capable of making up his own mind on the matter". Lord Bridge of Harwich agreed. Lord Fraser found no provision preventing him from holding that a girl under 16 lacked the legal capacity to consent to contraceptive advice and treatment provided "she had sufficient understanding and intelligence to know what they involve". Even Lord Templeman, who dissented, agreed that it was possible for a child to have capacity to consent to medical (but not contraceptive) treatment under the age of 16.

The case concerned the (then) parental right to consent to medical treatment, more specifically contraceptive treatment, but it is clear from the comments of various members of the court quoted above that they were wide enough to cover all (then) parental rights. Thus it was arguable that all parental rights ceased as and when the child had the capacity to make the decision himself. In the light of the **C.A.** shifting the emphasis from rights to responsibilities, there is an argument that parental responsibility terminates when the child has the capacity to make decisions himself.

The Court of Appeal had taken a very narrow and restrictive approach to the case, particularly in the area of medical treatment. In *Re R. (A Minor) (Wardship: Medical Treatment)* (1992) the court held that it had power under its parens patriae jurisdiction to override the decision of a competent child. It also said that parents could overrule a refusal by a competent child. This was followed in *Re W* (1993) where the court ordered a 16-year-old anorexic girl to be treated and in *Re E (Minor: Medical Treatment)* (1993) where the court ordered medical treatment even where the parents and a 15-year-old boy refused blood transfusions on the grounds of deeply held religious beliefs.

However, most recently in *Mabon v Mabon* the courts seemed to have returned to *Gillick* principles.

MABON V MABON (2005)

The appellant children (C) appealed against the decision refusing their application to remove their guardian ad litem (B) as their representative in family proceedings. C's parents had separated, with the mother taking the three youngest children with her, while the father remained in the matrimonial home with C. The mother applied for residence orders, and the children were joined as parties to the action, represented by a guardian.

The three elder children aged 17, 15 and 13 asked to instruct a firm of solicitors to represent them. They submitted that the judge had taken into account a number of irrelevant factors, had repeatedly introduced welfare considerations as if the paramountcy principle applied, and had failed to treat each applicant separately. It was argued that each child had a right to express his views freely under the **United Nations Convention on the Rights of the Child 1989** art.12; that a child's right to private life under the **Human Rights Act 1998** Sch.1 Pt I art.8 demanded a respect for his personal autonomy; and that a child's right to family life under art.8 included a procedural right of participation in the court's decision making process.

Held: allowing the appeal, there were a number of factors that pointed strongly towards the grant of separate representation in the case. Without separate representation they would be excluded from knowledge of and participation in legal proceedings that affected them so fundamentally. They had been seen by a family practitioner who had no doubt as to the sufficiency of their understanding, which was hardly surprising given that they were articulate, educated and reasonably mature for their respective ages. The judge was plainly wrong to refuse their application.

Unless the courts were to fall out of step with similar societies as they safeguarded art.12 rights, they had to accept, in the case of articulate teenagers, that the right to freedom of expression and participation outweighed the paternalistic judgment of welfare. In testing the sufficiency of a child's understanding it could not be said that welfare had no place. If direct participation would pose an obvious risk of harm to the child arising out of the nature of the continued proceedings, then the judge was entitled to find that sufficient understanding had not been demonstrated. But judges had to be equally alive to the risk of emotional harm that might arise from denying the child knowledge of and participation in the proceedings. CA said that the instant case provided a timely opportunity to recognise the growing acknowledgement of the autonomy and consequential rights of children, both nationally and internationally.

The decision has been welcomed as many commentators thought that previous CA decisions had been unfairly restrictive of mature children's rights.

The exercise of parental responsibility

By now, it will be appreciated that two or more persons may share parental responsibility. For example, parents married when the child was born share parental responsibility (see above). A third party may obtain a court order— one of the effects of which is to give him parental responsibility and, as this, save for an adoption order, does not terminate the parental responsibility of anyone who already has it (see above), shared parental responsibility will be created.

Section 2(7) provides that where parental responsibility is shared, each person having parental responsibility can act alone (subject to any enactment that provides for the consent of all on any specific issue).

Two general limitations to this freedom must be noted. First, if there comes into existence an order under the **C.A.** (which determines the way in which some part of parental responsibility may be exercised), the persons having parental responsibility may not act in any way that is incompatible with it (s.2(8)). For example, the court can grant a residence order under the **C.A.**, an order determining with whom the child is to live. If such an order is made, then a person with parental responsibility, who is not named in the order, can no longer exercise his parental responsibility by having the child live with him.

Secondly, despite s.2(7), it may be impossible in practice for one person with parental responsibility to exercise it without the co-operation of others with whom he shares it. For example, in practice, a married but separated father will find it impossible to exercise most aspects of his parental responsibility without the agreement of his wife, if the child lives with her. He will need the intervention of the court, thus bringing into play s.2(8).

. . . .

CHILDREN OF THE FAMILY

By s.105, the term "a child of the family", in relation to the parties to a marriage, means:

(a) a child of both parties; and
(b) any other child, not being a child who is placed with the parties as

foster parents ... who has been treated by both of the parties as a child of their family.

This definition appears also in the **Matrimonial Causes Act 1973** and the Domestic Proceedings and Magistrates' Courts Act 1978.

It will be seen that this is a relationship between a child and adults who are married to each other. The adults could be the child's natural parents but they need not be. One of the adults could be a parent and the other not: or both adults could have no blood tie with the child at all.

The relationship is of significance in that financial awards can be made in favour of such a child against the adults (Ch.4). The relationship does not result in the adults having parental responsibility for the child; if the adults, or one of them, are the child's parents, they or he will have parental responsibility due to parenthood not as a result of the child being a child of the family. But the existence of this relationship does give adults who are not the child's parents some preferential treatment: they are entitled to apply for some of the **C.A.** orders (see Ch.6).

Where it is necessary to prove that a child has been "treated as a child of the family", the issue is a question of fact to be viewed objectively. But there must be a family in existence before a child can be so treated:

A v A (HC 1974)
Prior to the marriage, the wife falsely told the husband that the child she was carrying was his. They married but parted before the child's birth.

Held: the child was not a child of the family.

PRINCIPLES USED BY THE COURTS TO DETERMINE DISPUTES

The non-intervention principle
By s.1(5), the court is enjoined not to make an order under the **C.A.** unless it considers that doing so would be better for the child than making no order at all. It is felt that it is better for the child if the parents can agree on the arrangements for him or her.

While the possibility of granting orders relating to the upbringing of children recognises that court intervention will be necessary on occasion, the non-intervention principle places a statutory "brake" upon it.

The Welfare principle

LEGISLATION HIGHLIGHTER

When determining any question relating to a child's upbringing or the administration of his property or income the most fundamental principle is that the child's welfare is the court's paramount consideration (s.1(1)).

BIRMINGHAM CITY COUNCIL V H (A MINOR) (NO.2) (1993)
The Local Authority had taken into care a child, aged two, whose mother, aged 16, was also in care, and proposed to terminate contact, contrary to the wishes of the mother. The House of Lords held unanimously that the child's welfare was paramount and for the purpose of these proceedings the mother was to be treated as the parent, not as another child who was also subject to the welfare principle.

KEY CASE

Here is Lord McDermott's attempt to define the meaning of "paramount" in *J v C* (HC 1969)

> "The words must mean more than that the child's welfare is to be treated as the top item in a list of items relevant to the matter in question. I think that they connote a process whereby when all relevant facts, relationships, claims and wishes of the parents, risks, choices and other circumstances are taken into account and weighed, the course to be followed will be that which is most in the interests of the child's welfare as that term has now to be understood. That is the paramount consideration because it rules on or determines the course to be followed".

Arguably, s.1(1), drawing on Lord McDermott's definition, means that the child's welfare is the determining or ruling factor, when dealing with questions relating to his upbringing or property.

THE WELFARE CHECKLIST

While of immense importance, the principle contained in s.1(1) is very widely drawn. For more specific guidance, the courts must take into account the statutory list of guidelines contained in s.1(3), which, by and large, enacts in statutory form the principles developed previously by the courts in case law.

Figure 10: The welfare checklist

The ascertainable wishes and feelings of the child
His physical, emotional and educational needs
The likely effect of change
Age, sex and background
Risk of harm
Capability of parents and any other person the court considers relevant
Range of powers available to the court

The checklist can be considered in more detail:

(a) the ascertainable wishes and feelings of the child (considered in the light of his age and understanding)—if at all, these used to be ascertained by a welfare officer, who had been ordered to prepare a report for the court;

(b) his physical, emotional and educational needs. Courts have long been influenced by the idea that a child's development is assisted by maintaining a relationship with both parents, if possible. However, this has usually been achieved by the courts ordering that a child should live with one parent and have frequent and regular contact with the other. Only exceptionally, have courts ordered the child to live with one for part of the time and the other for the rest.

Also, generally, it has not been considered beneficial to grant an order the effect of which would have been to split siblings;

(c) the likely effect on him of any change in his circumstances. Stability in the life of a child is considered beneficial. Thus, generally, a court has leant against an order the effect of which would have been to change well-established and beneficial arrangements, e.g. a change of home; a change of carer;

RE H (A MINOR) (CUSTODY: INTERIM CARE AND CONTROL) (CA 1991)
A divorced mother had died and her daughter, aged eight, was with the maternal grandmother. The trial judge had ordered the child to be returned to the father but the Appeal Court held that she would stay with the grandmother for the time being until a full investigation be completed. It was important for her to be close to the mother's relatives in the early stages of bereavement. Approved in *Re W (Residence Order)* (CA 1993).

(d) his age, sex, background and any characteristics of his which the court considers relevant—on the whole, courts have tended to consider that children need their mothers, young ones and girls in particular.

In *Re W (A Minor) (Residence Order)* (CA 1992) the court was prepared to say that there was a rebuttable presumption that a baby's best interest was to be with the mother. But in contrast, *Re S (A Minor) (Custody)* (CA 1991) it was held that there was no presumption that one parent should be preferred to another;

(e) any harm he has suffered or is at risk of suffering. Likely physical harm is obviously relevant but so is emotional harm. Thus, a parent's religious views or sexual preferences have been relevant if the court felt that they would damage the child. If the harm is "significant", it may trigger proceedings under Pt IV (see Ch.8);

(f) how capable each of his parents, and any other person in relation to whom the court considers the question to be relevant, is of meeting his needs. This factor has been considered relevant in relation to any new partner of the parents or other persons who would take a large part in the upbringing of the child; and

(g) the range of powers available to the court under the **C.A.** in the proceedings in question.

These factors must be taken into account by all courts when considering an application for the grant, variation or discharge of a s.8 order (see Ch.7) or an order under Pt IV of the **C.A.** (see Ch.8). Depending on the nature of the proceedings, some will be given more weight than others.

Delay
By s.1(2), the courts must take into account the principle that delay in resolving any dispute is likely to be prejudicial to a child.

CHILDREN'S RIGHTS

Despite the heavy emphasis in the current law on the role that adults play in the lives of children, there have already been a number of moves to acknowledge that children have a role to play in their own lives.

The case of *Gillick v West Norfolk Area Health Authority* has already been referred to above. The Lords therein acknowledged that in some circumstances a child had the right to determine whether or not she should have contraceptive advice and treatment and in language that indicated that children possibly had other rights too.

However, although the **C.A.** contains a number of provisions that allow children to make decisions for themselves, notably, the child's wishes and feelings under s.1(3) and the right to apply, with leave, for orders in respect of himself, the overriding principle of the **C.A.** is that decisions be taken with the child's welfare as the paramount consideration. The **H.R.A.** gives everyone the right to respect for his private and family life, his home and his correspondence. Children are not treated as children under the Convention, simply as persons. It has been thought that the principle of paramountcy may be problematic, but there are decisions of the European Court of Human Rights recognising the principle in other countries.

CA in *Mabon* (see above) have acknowledged our relationship with European Court of Human Rights.

Revision Checklist

By now you should know and understand:

- **the concept of Parental Responsibility and who has it or can obtain it**
- **the principles of "Gillick Competence"**
- **the all important Welfare Principle and the checklist in s.1**

QUESTION AND ANSWER

The Question

Chris and Gaby were married in 1994. After several miscarriages, Gaby was told that she could not carry a baby full term. Chris and Gaby then entered into an agreement with Gaby's married sister Kathy, that Kathy would bear a child for £10,000 "expenses".

An egg from Gaby was fertilised by sperm from Chris and the

embryo was then entered into an agreement with Gaby's married sister Kathy, that Kathy would bear a child for £10,000 "expenses".

An egg from Gaby was fertilised by sperm from Chris and the embryo was then implanted and carried full term by Kathy. Immediately after the birth, Kathy took the baby to Chris and Gaby. A year later, they were divorced on the grounds of Gaby's adultery with Danny. The baby lives with Gaby and Danny, who wants to apply for a residence order.

Chris, Kathy and her husband all want the baby to live with them respectively.

Advise the parties.

Suggested Answer

The question concerns Parental Responsibility (PR) and orders available under **H.F.E.A.** and **C.A.**

By virtue of s.28 of the **H.F.E.A.** the woman who gives birth is the mother and has automatic PR. If her husband consents to her treatment, he is the father. If not, the donor is the father but without PR.

C and G could have applied for a s.30 Order under **H.F.E.A.** to become parents, but all the conditions have to be complied with so they are out of time (must be within six months of birth) and the payment may be more than reasonable expenses.

A s.8 residence order will give PR to those who do not have it. C, G and D will need leave, K and her husband do not, but despite having PR will need to apply for an order to obtain residence.

The welfare principle applies to all proceedings and the court will use the checklist. The probable outcome would be for the child to remain with G, who has been her continuing carer.

RESOLUTION OF DISPUTES CONCERNING THE UPBRINGING OF CHILDREN BETWEEN PRIVATE INDIVIDUALS

7

INTRODUCTION

Prior to the **C.A.** 1989, the law was extremely complex. There was a wide variety of jurisdictions available, each relating to a specific situation, with its own procedures and types of orders. Further, the legal effect of the orders available was often unclear. The 1989 Act is designed to eradicate the complexity and uncertainty, yet still retain the flexibility, of the old law. In this chapter, references to section numbers are to those in the **C.A.** 1989, unless otherwise stated.

Save for adoption and an order warding a child, all former orders that related to the upbringing of children have been swept away by the Act.

1. A new guardianship scheme has been created by ss.5 and 6.
2. A new parental responsibility order for unmarried fathers has been created by s.4.
3. Most important, there are four orders, created by s.8 dealing with children's issues and referred to in the Act as "s.8 orders".

However, no proceedings can be commenced unless the parties have attended a Mediation Information and Assessment Meeting (MIAM) under the draft Bill 2012.

SECTION 8 ORDERS

Figure 11: The s.8 orders

Residence order
Contact order
Prohibited steps order
Specific issue order

The residence order

This is an order settling the arrangements to be made as to the person with whom the child is to live. It replaces the old "custody orders". It can be made in favour of anyone, save for a local authority. It can also be made in favour of more than one person, and if it is and those persons do not live together, then the order may specify the periods of time that the child is to spend with each of the persons named in the order.

It will frequently be the case that a residence order is granted to a person who already has parental responsibility for the child, e.g. a married parent. If this is not the case, the legal effect of the residence order is to give the person named in the order the parental responsibility for the child, save that such a person cannot consent to adoption or an order freeing for adoption or appoint a guardian (s.12). Such parental responsibility lasts as long as the residence order remains in force.

Obtaining a residence order is one way therefore for non-parents to obtain the parental responsibility (or at least the large part of it), for a child. If this happens however, remember that this does not destroy the parental responsibility that other persons e.g. the parents already have (s.2(6)): it means simply that they cannot act in any way that is incompatible with the residence order (s.2(8)).

The contact order

This is an order requiring the person with whom the child lives to allow the child to visit or stay, or otherwise have contact, with the person(s) named in the order. It replaces "Access Orders". Again, it can be made in favour of anyone, save for a local authority. The term "or otherwise have contact with" is capable of wide interpretation and could include for example writing to or receiving from, or making or receiving telephone calls to or from, the named person.

Contact orders have been notoriously difficult to enforce. Failing to obey the order is clearly contempt of court, which is usually punished by imprisonment. But incarcerating the child's carer is obviously not in the child's best interests.

The **Children and Adoption Act 2006** (which came into force in December 2008) offers the courts new and more flexible powers, including:

(a) Power to direct parties in a contact case to attend information meetings, meetings with a counsellor, parenting programmes or classes or other activities designed to deal with contact disputes; and

(b) Power to attach conditions to contact orders which may require attendance at a given class or programme.

Where a contact order has been breached, courts will be able to:

(a) impose community-based "enforcement orders" for unpaid work or curfew; or

(b) award financial compensation from one party to another (for example where the cost of a holiday has been lost). The Act has been criticised for criminalising mothers who breach contact orders. It has also been said that it could encourage parties to continue disputes about contact rather than reduce or eliminate them.

Reform

Under the draft Bill 2012 residence and contact orders are to be abolished and replaced by a Child Arrangements Order defined as an order regulating arrangements relating to any of the following.

(a) with whom a child is to live, spend time or otherwise have contact; and

(b) when a child is to live, spend time or otherwise have contact with any person.

Such orders are available to unmarried fathers and family members such as siblings and grandparents. The Family Justice Review considered that the old orders still contained an element of "winning and losing" in the eyes of litigant parents.

The following orders still remain:

The prohibited steps order

This is an order directing a person named in the order not to take a specified step in relation to the child without the consent of the court. It can be made against anyone.

The "specified step" must be one which could be taken by a parent in meeting his parental responsibility. Thus, for example, any person could be directed not to make contact with the child or remove him from this country.

The specific issues order

This is an order that determines a specific question in connection with any aspect of parental responsibility, for example which school the child should attend, whether or not medical treatment should be given, see, for example, *Re HG (Specific Issue: Sterilisation)* (1993) and *Re R. (A minor) (Blood Transfusion)* (1993).

Neither the prohibited steps order nor the specific issues order can be made with a view to achieving a result which could be achieved by the making of a residence or contact order (s.9(5)). If this provision were not on the statute book, a person could feasibly avoid the legal effect of the residence or contact order by seeking a specific issue or prohibited steps order to cover the same situation.

All s.8 orders can be made subject to directions as to their implementation and conditions that must be complied with (s.11(7)). For example, it would be possible to grant a person a residence order subject to the condition that he lived in a named town; or subject to a condition that he provide regular reports on the progress of the child at school to some other person. The contact order could include precise directions as to the place, manner and time of the visits.

None of these orders can be made once the child has reached his sixteenth birthday or extend beyond that date, unless there are exceptional circumstances (s.9(6) and (7)). In any event, all of these orders cease automatically when the child reaches 18 (s.9(11)).

TYPES OF PROCEEDINGS

Disputes concerning the upbringing of children can arise in many ways. The adults in dispute could be in dispute solely over the upbringing of the child: or they may also be in dispute about other matters (e.g. divorce) that can be conveniently linked with the dispute over the child.

The **C.A.** 1989 sweeps away virtually all the mass of previous statutory provisions relating to the upbringing of children. Now, the only way for private individuals to take the initiative to resolve a dispute concerning the upbringing of a child is for one of them to issue proceedings under the **C.A.** The only exceptions relate to wardship and adoption orders.

Under s.5, it is possible to apply for an order appointing a guardian of the child, such an order giving parental responsibility. It is also possible for an unmarried father to apply for an order giving him parental responsibility (s.4—see Ch.6). However, the main type of application possible is for a s.8 order.

An application for a s.8 order can be made in one of two ways:

1. as a free standing application (s.10(2)); or
2. as part of "family proceedings" (s.10(1)).

"Family proceedings" are defined in s.8, as amended by s.63 of the **Family Law Act 1986**. The list includes proceedings under the **M.C.A. 1973**, the **D.P.M.C.A. 1978**, the **A.C.A. 2002** and the **F.L.A. 1996** (including Pt IV). It also includes applications under the **C.A. 1989** itself. So, for example, if an unmarried father brings a s.4 application, s.8 orders can be sought and made in those proceedings.

It should also be noted that once family proceedings are issued, the court can make a s.8 order of its own motion (s.10(1)).

CATEGORIES OF APPLICANTS

Usually, it is the parents of a child who are in dispute about his upbringing. However, this is not always necessarily so; a person who has no relationship whatsoever with the child may still have a genuine interest in his welfare and require an order relating to his upbringing.

The **C.A.** recognises the need for persons other than parents of a child to be able to obtain orders relating to his upbringing. It would have been possible to provide that any one was entitled to apply for a s.8 order. However, this freedom was not considered appropriate and the Act lays down categories of applicant in s.10.

Figure 12: Who can apply for a s.8 order?

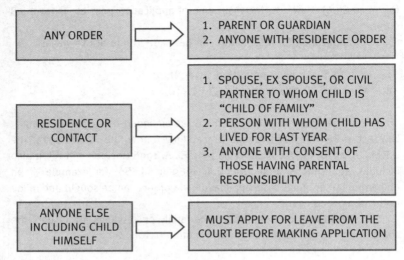

1. Those entitled to apply for any s.8 order:
    (i) a parent or guardian of the child (it need not be a parent with parental responsibility); and
    (ii) a person who has been granted a residence order.
2. Those entitled to apply for a Child Arrangements order:
    (i) a spouse or ex-spouse or civil partner in relation to whom the child is a child of the family (see Ch.6);
    (ii) a person with whom the child has lived for at least one year (amended by the Children and Young Persons Act 2008). S.10(10) provides that this need not be continuous, so long as the period does not commence more than five years, nor end more than three months before the making of the application; and
    (iii) a person who has the consent of:
        (a) the person in whose favour there is a residence order, if one has been granted;
        (b) the local authority, if the child is in care; or
        (c) in any other case, every person with parental responsibility.
3. Any other person who has leave of the court to make the application.

The matters which a court must take into account on an application for leave are designed to prevent frivolous and/or harmful applications for s.8 orders being made. They include the nature of the applicant's connection with the child (s.10(9)) but as it is not "a question with respect to the upbringing of the child", his or her welfare is not a paramount consideration. An unusual example is:

> RE A AND OTHERS (MINORS) (RESIDENCE ORDERS: LEAVE TO APPLY) (CA 1992)
> Six disturbed children (aged 9–14) had been taken into care and placed with an experienced but strong-minded foster mother. The arrangement worked for two years, then the two elder children ran away. The other four were taken for assessment, then placed with another foster family. The first foster mother applied for leave to apply for residence orders. The Court of Appeal refused. The court could assume that the Local Authority were safeguarding the children's welfare; they and the natural mother opposed the application, the children did not want to go back, and no point would be served in a lengthy and bitter court battle.

THE RELATIONSHIP BETWEEN THE PRIVATE AND THE PUBLIC LAW

In Ch.8, there is discussed the topic of protection of a child by local authority intervention in his life. This topic can no longer be studied as if it were a completely separate topic from the law discussed in this chapter: the two interweave.

As seen above, two of the s.8 orders, the specific issue order and the prohibited steps order can be granted in favour of a local authority.

Further, as will be seen in Ch.8, a local authority can apply for care or supervision orders, under Pt IV of the **C.A.** Such an application is included in the definition of "family proceedings". Thus, if such an application is initiated, an application for a s.8 order can be made, or the court can make a s.8 order of its own motion, within it.

The circle does not end here however: as will be seen, applications for care and supervision orders can be made within family proceedings. Thus, a private individual who has instituted some form of family proceedings in which a question relating to a child arises, may find a local authority applying within them for care or supervision.

This interweaving is an attempt to ensure that the courts have the powers to resolve an issue relating to a child in the most appropriate way, without being limited by the identity of the applicant or the nature of the order sought.

By now you should know and understand:

- the available orders under s.8 and their respective applications
- the persons who may apply for such orders

QUESTION AND ANSWER

The Question

C, a girl aged 14, has been raped and is now 10 weeks pregnant. She is suffering severe shock and will not talk to anyone about her situation, save that she says she wants an abortion. Since her parents' divorce, C has lived with her mother, Mrs X but sees her father, Mr X regularly. On the divorce, Mrs X obtained a residence order in respect of C. Mrs X has deep rooted objections to abortion: Mr X does not.

Is it necessary to obtain the consent of Mrs X to an abortion?

Suggested Answer

Can C consent to the abortion herself? **Family Law Reform Act 1969** allows 16-year-olds to do so but as she is below that age she must rely on *Gillick*. C must be capable "of understanding what is proposed" and the operation is "best for her welfare". Does she have "sufficient intelligence, understanding and maturity to understand?" (per Lord Scarman). Note that the CA in *Re R.* and *Re W* has taken a different, restrictive view. Can C find assistance from the **C.A.**?

She is born to married parents so both have joint Parental Responsibility (PR) (s.2(1)). Both can exercise PR but neither can act in a way incompatible with any order granted under the **C.A.** (s.2(8)). Although Mrs X has a s.8 Residence Order, Mr X can legally consent but it may be practically impossible for the operation to be carried out as C lives with her mother. The solution may be for Mr X to apply for a specific issue order under s.8 asking for a direction that the abortion be carried out. He is entitled to apply under s.9(4). If granted, Mrs X must not act in a way incompatible with the order.

PROTECTION OF CHILDREN— LOCAL AUTHORITY INTERVENTION AND WARDSHIP

8

INTRODUCTION

Occasionally, the State is forced to intervene between a child and its carers, either to remove the child completely from the home or to provide some form of intermediate protection. Usually the protection is achieved by means of local authority intervention in the life of the child, but protection can also be given by making a child a ward of court. References in this chapter to section numbers are to those in the **C.A. 1989**, unless otherwise stated.

Prior to the enactment of the **C.A.**, there were many different types of orders available to a local authority to enable it to offer protection to a child.

The Act introduces:

1. orders which enable a local authority to act in emergencies and to make investigations;
2. care and supervision orders.

It should be carefully noted that the latter orders can only be made if the "Threshold Criteria" under s.31(2) has been met (see below).

Section 47 Local authority's duty to investigate

(1) Where a local authority—

   (a) are informed that a child who lives, or is found, in their area—

      (i) is the subject of an emergency protection order; or

      (ii) is in police protection; or

      (iii) has contravened a ban imposed by a curfew notice within the meaning of Ch.I of Pt I of the Crime and Disorder Act 1998; or

   (b) have reasonable cause to suspect that a child who lives, or is found, in their area is suffering, or is likely to suffer, significant harm, the authority shall make, or cause to be made, such enquiries as they consider necessary to enable them to decide whether they should take any action to safeguard or promote the child's welfare.

In the case of a child falling within paragraph (a)(iii) above, the enquiries shall be commenced as soon as practicable.

If, on the conclusion of any enquiries or review made under this section, the authority decide not to apply for an emergency protection order, a child assessment order, a care order or a supervision order they shall—

(a) consider whether it would be appropriate to review the case at a later date; and

(b) if they decide that it would be, determine the date on which that review is to begin.

Where, as a result of complying with this section, a local authority conclude that they should take action to safeguard or promote the child's welfare they shall take that action (so far as it is both within their power and reasonably practicable for them to do so).

TYPES OF ORDERS

The orders that are available are as follows:

1. the care order (s.31);
2. the supervision order (s.31);
3. the education supervision order (s.36);
4. the emergency protection order (s.44); and
5. the child assessment order (s.43).

Section 6 of the **H.R.A. 1998** makes it unlawful for a public authority to act in a way incompatible with the Convention. Clearly local authorities fall within this section and they must be on their guard to ensure that art.6 (right to a fair hearing) is complied with. In exercise of their powers affecting art.8 (right to family life) the House of Lords have already ruled that a local authority did not infringe parents' rights when their child was taken into care: the authority were carrying out its duties to protect the child under the exceptions to art.8.

Figure 13: Use of the orders

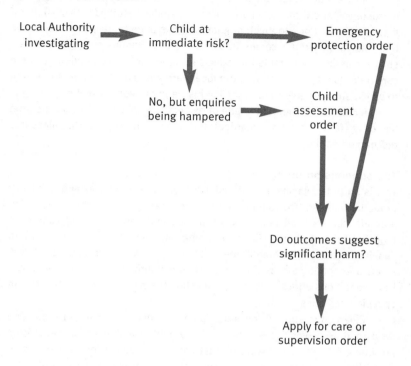

The care order

This is an order that commits a child into the care of a local authority. It cannot be made in favour of anyone else.

The practical effect of a care order is that the child goes to live in a local authority community home or with local authority foster parents.

Under the draft Bill 2012 applications must proceed:

(i)   without delay, and
(ii)   in any event within 26 weeks beginning with the day on which the application was issued; there are limited exceptions but this is a very controversial proposal.

The legal effect of a care order is that the local authority obtains parental responsibility for the child so long as the care order is in force (s.33(3)). It cannot, however, cause the child to be brought up in any religious persuasion other than that in which he would have been brought up if the order had not been made. Nor can it consent to an order for adoption or freeing for adoption or appoint a guardian (s.33(6)).

A care order automatically brings to an end any residence order that is in existence, and with it any parental responsibility that it gave (s.9(2)). But if a parent (natural or adoptive), or guardian, has parental responsibility at the time that a care order comes into force, this continues (s.2(6)). However, such a person is not entitled to exercise it in any way incompatible with the care order (s.2(8)) and, further, the local authority may determine the extent to which such a person may exercise his parental responsibility.

A care order cannot be made in respect of a child who has reached the age of 17 (16, if the child is married). It lasts until the child is 18, unless it is discharged earlier.

The supervision order

This is an order placing a child under the supervision of a local authority or probation officer. The supervision order does not give the supervising authority the parental responsibility for the child and the child cannot be removed from his home. The supervising authority merely has the duty to "advise, assist and befriend" the child, which it will do in any way it considers appropriate, e.g. by visiting the child regularly. A supervision order can have conditions attached to it, e.g. directing the participation of the child in specified activities.

Clearly, the supervision order is an intermediate means of protection for a child. However, if the supervising authority considers that the order is not being fully complied with, it must consider applying for its variation or discharge and, if the latter, may also consider applying for a care order.

A supervision order cannot be made in respect of a child who has reached the age of 17 (16, if the child is married). Generally, a supervision order lasts for one year. It can be extended for up to a further two years. In any event, it cannot extend beyond the child's eighteenth birthday.

The education supervision order

This is an order placing a child under the supervision of a local education authority. Like the supervision order, it does not give the authority parental responsibility for the child.

The emergency protection order

Proceedings for the orders previously referred to will usually take some time to conclude. Some children require protection more quickly and the emergency protection order is designed to fulfil this need.

It is an order that authorises a local authority (or the N.S.P.C.C.) to remove a child from his home and gives it parental responsibility. Regulations provide that an application for an emergency protection order can be made without notice; that is, without the necessity to inform the child's parents or any other person that the application is about to be made. Thus, it will be possible to obtain the order very swiftly indeed and after the court has heard only the local authority's side of the case.

This order lasts for only eight days, and can only be extended once by a further period not exceeding seven days. Further, after 72 hours, an application for its discharge can be made (s.45(1), (5), (6) and (9)). In addition, it is specifically provided that the local authority shall only take such action in meeting its parental responsibility as is reasonably required to safeguard or promote the welfare of the child (s.44(5)).

The child assessment order
Sometimes, a local authority fears that a child may be at immediate risk, yet, because it cannot gain access to the child, has no real evidence of the fact or extent of the risk. The child assessment order provides a solution to this dilemma in a non-emergency situation.

The child assessment order has effect for no more than seven days (s.43(5)) and authorises either a local authority or the N.S.P.C.C. to carry out an assessment on the child (s.43(7)). Any person who is in a position to produce the child for assessment must do so (s.43(6)). To give added strength to the order, it is provided that a child assessment order may permit the removal of the child from his home (s.43(9)). By virtue of s.43(8) if the child is of sufficient understanding to make an informed decision, he may refuse to submit to the assessment. The child assessment order does not give the local authority or the N.S.P.C.C. parental responsibility for the child.

The intention is to enable the local authority to assess the child, so that it can better make its decision as to whether to apply for further orders, yet, at the same time, cause the minimum harm to the child.

. . . .

TYPES OF PROCEEDINGS

Subject to a very limited use of the wardship jurisdiction (see below), the **C.A.** is now the only jurisdiction under which a local authority may intervene in the life of a child.

However, a certain amount of flexibility is retained, by sometimes permitting the use of the same device as has been discussed in Ch.8. By s.31(4), an application for a care order or a supervision order can be made on its own or within family proceedings, as defined by s.8(3) (see Ch.8). However, applications for education supervision orders, emergency protection orders and child assessment orders may only be made as free standing applications and not within family proceedings.

CATEGORIES OF APPLICANT

The wide scope that prevails within the sphere of resolution of private disputes was not thought appropriate for this area and the categories of persons who are entitled to apply for the above orders for the protection of children are extremely limited:

1. Care orders, supervision orders and child assessment orders: only a local authority or the N.S.P.C.C. may apply.
2. Education supervision orders: only a local education authority may apply.
3. Emergency protection orders: any person may apply. (The emergency nature and limited life of this order should be remembered. In practice, it will most often be sought by a local authority.)

Further it has been considered correct not to re-enact the court's previous powers to make orders for the protection of children of its own motion. Thus, even if a court dealing with private law family proceedings feels that, e.g. a care order should be made in respect of a child, it cannot make such an order unless the local authority applies for one within those proceedings.

In place of the previous powers to make orders of its own motion, the court now has more intermediate powers under s.37. Where a court is dealing with family proceedings in which a question relating to the welfare of a child arises, it may direct a local authority to investigate the child's circumstances, if it appears that a care or supervision order may be appropriate. Once so directed, a local authority has the duty to carry out an investigation, and to consider, inter alia, whether it should apply for a care or supervision order. If it decides not to, a local authority must report this to the court. However, there is nothing the court can do to reverse the local authority decision.

THE RELATIONSHIP BETWEEN THE PUBLIC AND PRIVATE LAW

As has been stated earlier, care and supervision orders can be sought by a local authority and granted, within proceedings initially instituted by a private individual to resolve a dispute between himself and another private individual, so long as such proceedings fall within the definition of family proceedings.

Further, what by now may have been forgotten, is that a local authority may, with leave, apply for and be granted a specific issue order or a prohibited steps order, either as a freestanding application or within family proceedings (see Ch.7).

Finally, applications for care orders, supervision orders and education supervision orders are themselves "family proceedings" (s.8(4)). Thus, whenever such an application is made, the applicant (the local authority, N.S.P.C.C. or education local authority) must face the fact that the court has the power to grant a specific issue order or prohibited steps order instead of the order sought, or indeed, a s.8 order to a private individual.

THRESHOLD CRITERIA

LEGISLATION HIGHLIGHTER

Care and supervision orders (s.31(2))
The court has to be satisfied:

(a) that the child is suffering or likely to suffer significant harm; and
(b) that the harm or likelihood of harm is attributable to:
  (i) the care given to the child, or likely to be given to him if the order were not made, not being what it would be reasonable to expect a parent to give to him; or
  (ii) the child's being beyond parental control.

Establishing the grounds in s.31(2) is necessary to enable the court to make a care or supervision order. The court does not have to: indeed, before it does, there are other matters that it must take into account, that may lead it to refuse such orders. As a result, the matters specified in s.31(2) are popularly called "the threshold criteria".

The phrase "is suffering" was the subject of interpretation by the House of Lords in:

RE M (CARE ORDER: THRESHOLD CONDITIONS) (1994)
Baby M's mother was murdered by his father. He was accommodated initially by the Local Authority, who started care proceedings, and then moved to a relative who was already caring for his brothers and sisters. She applied for a residence order and by the time the case came to appeal, M was flourishing. It was argued that he was no longer "suffering".

Held: the relevant time is when the Local Authority initiated "protective arrangements" not the date of the hearing. A care order was made, though in fact M continued living with his relative.

"Harm" is defined in s.31(9) as "ill treatment, or the impairment of health or development" and those terms are defined in the same subsection. In short, it is not only the child's physical well being that is protected. It is further provided that, where the harm alleged is "impairment of health or development", whether or not it is significant shall be decided by using the standard of the health or development to be reasonably expected of a similar child (s.31(10)).

Predicting future harm under "likely to suffer" is also not without its difficulties. In *Re H (Minors) (Sexual Abuse: Standard of Proof)* (1996) the House of Lords held that there must be a real possibility of harm which cannot sensibly be ignored. This is not easy, particularly when considering a child's long-term development.

The whole of s.1 applies to care and supervision proceedings. This is discussed in Ch.7 under the heading "Principles to be applied by the courts when determining disputes".

Education supervision orders (ss.36(3) and (4))

The court has to be satisfied that the child is of compulsory school age and is not being properly educated: i.e. receiving efficient full-time education, suitable to his age, ability, aptitude and any special education needs he may have.

Again, proof of this ground can be looked upon as having reached a threshold only. Applications for education supervision orders are subject to the whole of s.1.

Emergency protection orders (s.44(1))

Three situations are catered for under the **C.A. 1989**: applications made by a local authority or the N.S.P.C.C., where either of them is already making enquiries into a child's welfare, and any other application.

To summarise:

(a) a local authority, already making enquiries, must show merely that the enquiries are being frustrated and that access to the child is required as a matter of urgency;

(b) the N.S.P.C.C., already making enquiries, must show the matters mentioned in (a), plus that it has reasonable cause to suspect that the child is suffering, or likely to suffer, significant harm; and

(c) any other applicant must show that there is reasonable cause to believe that the child is likely to suffer significant harm if he is not removed to other accommodation.

Again, proof of the ground can be looked upon as having reached a threshold only. Applications for emergency protection orders are subject to the provisions of s.1, save for s.1(3), the statutory list of guidelines. It will be remembered that these orders are for the emergency protection of children: it was not thought appropriate to insist that the courts should take note of these matters on what were likely to be speedy applications.

Child assessment orders (s.43(1))
To summarise, the court has to be satisfied that:

(a) the applicant has reasonable cause to suspect that the child is suffering or likely to suffer significant harm;
(b) this can only be determined by an assessment of the child's health or development; and
(c) it is not likely that an assessment will be made without an order.

Again, proof of the ground can be regarded as having reached a threshold only. Applications for child assessment orders are subject to the provisions of s.1, save for s.1(3). Such applications are, again, emergency applications.

PARENTAL CONTACT

By s.34, a local authority is placed under a duty to allow reasonable contact between a child in care and, inter alia, his parents. If there is a dispute as to what is reasonable, then the court can make such order for contact as it considers appropriate. In limited circumstances, a local authority can refuse to permit contact, for up to seven days.

By s.43, if a child is to be kept away from his home during the currency of a child assessment order, the order must contain directions for such contact between the child and other persons as the court thinks fit.

By s.44, an applicant who is granted an emergency protection order is placed under a duty to allow reasonable contact between the child, and inter alia, his parents.

CHILDREN ACT 2004

In September 2003, the Government published the *Every Child Matters* Green Paper alongside its formal response to the Victoria Climbié Inquiry Report. The Green Paper proposed changes in policy and legislation in England to maximise opportunities and minimise risks for all children and young people, focusing services more effectively around the needs of children, young people and families.

The consultation on the Green Paper showed broad support for the proposals, in particular the intention to concentrate on outcomes that children and young people themselves have said are important, rather than prescribing organisational change. The Act has been produced in the light of this consultation and gives effect to the legislative proposals set out in the Green Paper to create clear accountability for children's services, to enable better joint working and to secure a better focus on safeguarding children.

To ensure a voice for children and young people at national level, Pt 1 of the Act provides for the establishment of a Children's Commissioner ("the Commissioner").

The general function of the Commissioner is set out in s.1(1). The Commissioner is to promote awareness of the views and interests of children in England. As well as those under 18, the term "children" includes persons aged 18, 19 and 20 who have been looked after by a local authority at any time after attaining the age of 16 or who have a learning disability. He will be expected to raise the profile of the issues that affect and concern children in England, and promote awareness and understanding of their views and interests among all sectors of society, both public and private. The Commissioner will therefore be expected actively to gather and understand the views of children from all backgrounds. However, the Commissioner will also be expected to use his own judgement in determining the interests of children, which may not always be the same as their own expressed wishes, especially with younger children.

In carrying out his general function the Commissioner should have particular regard to the aspects of "well-being" set out in subs.(3)(a)–(e) namely:

(a) physical and mental health and emotional well-being;
(b) protection from harm and neglect;
(c) education, training and recreation;
(d) the contribution made by them to society;
(e) social and economic well-being.

These reflect the five outcomes which, during the development of the Green Paper *Every Child Matters*, children identified as being the most important to them. It is intended that they form the framework for the Commissioner's activities. Through carrying out his general function the Commissioner will monitor and stimulate progress towards achieving these outcomes for all children.

Section 1(7) prohibits the Commissioner from conducting investigations into individual cases. The intention is that this will allow him to concentrate on the broader issues that affect children. However, s.3 permits the Commissioner to initiate inquiries into individual cases that meet certain criteria.

The case concerned must raise issues of public policy that would be relevant to other children. This would for example mean that the Commissioner could hold an inquiry into the case of a child in a children's home or a residential school if the issues involved were relevant in general to children in such an establishment, but not if they were only relevant to children in that particular establishment.

Section 3 requires the Commissioner to consult the Secretary of State before holding an inquiry. The Secretary of State may offer guidance, but has no power to veto an inquiry: the final decision is for the Commissioner.

Section 4(1) enables the Secretary of State to direct the Commissioner to hold an inquiry into the case of an individual child, where the Secretary of State considers the case to be of wider relevance or have implications for other children. In contrast to the power under s.3, the Commissioner could under this section carry out an inquiry into a case which only has implications for a small group of children. E.g. he could hold an inquiry into the case of a child in a children's home or a residential school if the issues involved were relevant in general to children in such an establishment, or if they were only relevant to children in that particular establishment.

Section 10 requires Local Authorities to make arrangements to promote co-operation between the Authority its relevant partners and any other bodies working with children to improve the well being of children in their area.

Section 12 provides for the creation of a nationwide database of children suspected of neglect or abuse in families.

Despite the Inquiries and legislation, the *Baby Peter* case highlights the failings of the system in dealing with cases of abuse.

CHILDREN AND YOUNG PERSONS ACT 2008

The purpose of the Act, which came into force in September 2009, is to reform the statutory framework for the care system in England and in Wales to ensure that children and young people receive high quality care and to drive improvements in the delivery of services focused on the needs of the child.

The Act focuses on improving placement stability, educational experience and attainment and the transparency and quality of care planning. The Act seeks to ensure that young people are not forced out of care before they are ready, by giving them a greater say over moves to independent living and ensuring they retain support and guidance as long as they need it. It is not necessary for our purposes to go into any more detail but it will have significant implications for local government and will need careful planning and implementation.

WARDSHIP

Wardship is the means by which the family court fulfils its parens patriae jurisdiction, that is, the protection of children.

When a child becomes a ward of court, the court controls its upbringing by a series of directions and orders of the widest variety so long as the wardship lasts. Wardship not only deals with the issues of where and with whom a child shall live, but also with important other issues, for example, consenting to an operation to remove a potentially fatal intestinal blockage (*Re B* (CA 1981)): to perform an abortion (*Re P* (HC 1986)): to decide whether to prolong a dying baby's life or to ease his suffering (*Re C* (CA 1989)).

The flexibility of wardship also appealed to Local Authorities who often chose this jurisdiction in preference to care proceedings. The result was a dramatic increase in the number of cases during the two decades preceding the **C.A.**

However, by s.100 of the **C.A.**, no local authority may apply to make a child a ward of court unless it has leave of the court to do so. The grounds for leave are so limited that it seems wardship will be used in only the most exceptional circumstances. In the area of private law, the reduction in Legal Aid limits is likely to affect the number of applications, particularly as s.8 orders are available in the lower courts. Nonetheless, the immediacy of wardship and its ability to deal with unusual, if not unique, situations, means that wardship still has a role to play in child law.

X COUNTY COUNCIL v A (1985)

A notorious murderer, on release from prison, had changed her name and gone to live in a different part of the country. She had her child warded so that the court could order the News of the World not to publish any material which would identify either mother or child.

DEVON COUNTY COUNCIL v S (WARDSHIP) (1993)

S had three young children. She was regularly visited by X who had convictions for sexual offences. The local authority applied for wardship to protect the children. The trial judge refused, relying on s.10 but leave was granted by the Court of Appeal to enable contact between X and the children to be prevented, something which care or supervision orders could not achieve.

Re A (Conjoined Twins) 2001

The parents of conjoined twins refused to consent to their separation even though both would die. The children were made wards so that the operation could be undertaken, even though it meant the certain death of the weaker twin.

Revision Checklist

By now you should know and understand:

- **the role of and powers available to Local Authorities when concerned with children in need**
- **the meaning and importance of the "Threshold Criteria"**
- **the residual role of Wardship in public law**

QUESTION AND ANSWER

The Question

Freda lives in a council flat with her boyfriend Mark. Freda has two girls, aged eight and six, from a former relationship and a two-year-old boy with Mark. He is unemployed and has a serious drink problem. Freda works part time as a laptop dancer at a local club and when she works, Mark looks after the children. He frequently smacks them but as his drinking gets heavier, he has become abusive and threatening. Freda told a neighbour she would leave but has nowhere to go, and anyway, she still loves him. When the neighbour hears Mark shouting threats at the children and throwing empty beer cans at them, she telephones social services. A social worker calls shortly after Freda's return from work. Freda refuses to let her in or even talk to her.

Advise Freda.

Suggested Answer

The Local Authority (L.A.) can only act if the "Threshold Criteria" under s.31 are met, namely, are the children suffering or likely to suffer significant harm. Expand on the meanings of "harm" and "significant". As to likelihood see *Newham Borough Council* case. If Freda will not co-operate, the L.A. can ask for an Assessment order under s.33 or an Emergency Protection order under ss.44 and 45. Once the enquiries are complete, the L.A. can apply for a care order under s.37 which gives them PR in partnership with Freda.

The alternative is to remove Mark under the **C.A.** provisions amended by the **F.L.A.** with possibly a supervision order to ensure that Mark stays away.

Care proceedings are "family proceedings" for the purposes of the **C.A.** so the court can make any order available to it under the **C.A.** or even no order at all under s.1(5).

ADOPTION

INTRODUCTION

Adoption was first introduced into English law in 1926. The modern substantive law is now contained in the **A.C.A. 2002**. which received the Royal
Assent in October 2002 after a controversial passage through Parliament but
was not fully implemented until 2004. Adoption means that a child severs all
legal relationships with his or her natural parents and replaces them with a
new legal relationship with the adoptive parents though the court could, for
example, order that contact be maintained with the child's natural parents or
siblings. Adoption proceedings are family proceedings for the purposes of
the **C.A. 1989,** so the courts are empowered to make s.8 orders instead of
adoption if the court so thinks fit.

But once an Adoption order is made, it is final (s.46(2)(a)). The present
Government intends to legislate that the process should be completed in 12
months.

The effects of adoption

Section 12 of the **A.A. 1976**. provides that an adoption order gives parental
responsibility to the adoptive parents and any parental responsibility in
others, including the natural parents, is extinguished. Section 39 provides
that where the adopters are married to each other, the child shall be treated
as a legitimate child of the marriage. In any other case, the adopted child
shall not be treated as if he or she were illegitimate.

With regard to the rules of succession, an adopted child is entitled to
claim as a natural child of any adoptive parent who died after January 1, 1976
having made a will on or before that date, unless a contrary intention is
expressed. Section 47(1) provides that for the purposes of marriage and the
crime of incest, adoption does not affect the prohibited degrees of relationship which result from a child's birth to his or her natural parent.
Although an adopted child cannot marry his adoptive parent, he or she is
permitted to marry his or her adoptive sister or brother.

THE WELFARE PRINCIPLE

The **A.A. 1976** tried to strike a balance between parental rights to consent to adoption and the child's welfare in contrast to the **C.A. 1989** criteria which makes the child's welfare the paramount consideration. Section 1(2) of the **A.C.A. 2002** provides that the paramount consideration of the court must be the child's welfare throughout his life and includes similar provisions to the welfare checklist in the **C.A. 1989** reflecting the view of the then Government that adoption is a service for children.

Adoption Services

Section 3 of the **A.C.A. 2002** states that only Local Authorities or a registered adoption society can provide adoption services. Adoption agencies have responsibility for selecting and assessing adopters and placing children for adoption. Where the Local Authority wishes to place a child in care for adoption, it must produce a care plan setting out its plans for the child's future.

Who can adopt and be adopted?

The person to be adopted must:

(a) Be under 18: s.72(1) of the **A.A. 1976**.

(b) Be at least 10 weeks old and have had his home with the applicant at all times during the preceding 13 weeks, if either applicant is the child's parent, step parent or relative, or the child was placed with the applicant by an adoption agency or by order of the High Court.
If the applicant does not meet those criteria, then the child must be at least 12 months old and must have had his home with the applicant at all times during the preceding three years.

(c) Never have been married.

(d) Have parental agreement to the adoption.

Who may adopt?

(a) An adoptive parent must be at least 21 years of age. If the applicants are a parent and a step parent, the former must at least be 18 and the latter aged 21 or over.

(b) If a couple apply, they must be married or in "an enduring family relationship" s.51(3) of the **A.C.A. 2002**.

(c) An unmarried person may apply if they are aged 21 or over; a married person over the age of 21 and a sole applicant may apply if:

(i) his or her spouse cannot be found or, by virtue of the **H.F.E.A. 1990**, there is no other parent; or

(ii) the spouses are living apart and the separation is likely to be permanent; or

(iii) the other spouse is incapable of applying by reason of ill health, physical or mental, of applying for an order.

The adopters must also establish suitability. Section 45 of the **A.C.A. 2002** specifies two grounds:

(a) stability and permanence of the relationship (s.45(2)).

(b) religious persuasion, racial origin and cultural and linguistic background (s.1(5)).

"Matching" by this criteria is not an exact science and must be decided on a case by case basis.

Although the Act does not differentiate, there are different types of adoption, which involve their own particular and peculiar problems and difficulties. The child in question may be a complete stranger to the adopters. For example, publicity concerning unwanted children in Eastern European countries led to numbers of English couples making application for adoption and more famously, both Angelina Jolie and Madonna have adopted children from African countries.

Part 2 of the **Children and Adoption Act 2006** includes provisions relating to dealing with systems in some countries where there are insufficient safeguards in place to protect child welfare. The Act provides a statutory framework for the suspension of intercountry adoptions from specified countries where there are public policy concerns about the process in that country, such as child trafficking.

Step parent adoptions (although discouraged) are the most popular type of adoption. There is a new provision (s.112) which allows parental responsibility to be given to a step parent, similar to s.4 **C.A. 1989**. It is expected that this will replace adoption for them.

Relatives of the child (as defined) are able to adopt but the practice has been to grant s.8 Residence orders instead. The **A.C.A. 2002** builds on that by introducing a new "Special Guardian" (s.115).

Figure 14: Who may apply for special guardianship order?

Guardian of the child
Person with residence order
Anyone with consent of all those with parental responsibility
Any person with whom the child has lived for 3 out of the last 5 years
Local authority foster parent with whom child has lived for 1 year.

He or she will be given parental responsibility for the child and take day to day decisions concerning the child's upbringing. The natural parents remain the legal parents with restricted parental responsibility.

KEY CASE

RE S (ADOPTION OR SPECIAL GUARDIANSHIP ORDER) [2007]
Child aged six placed with foster-mother by Local Authority but mother and father still had contact. Foster mother applied for adoption but given S.G.O. instead. On appeal, CA confirmed that the welfare principle is over-riding concern and providing Judge has considered all the facts, then it is unlikely that the appeal courts will interfere.

Parental agreement

Each parent or guardian of a child must agree unconditionally to the making of an adoption order. The consent must be freely given, with full understanding of what is involved, and whether or not he or she knows the identity of the applicant.

The parent cannot impose conditions, although the court may do so under the powers given to it by the **A.C.A. 2002.** This could particularly apply to the child's religious upbringing. Section 7 requires adoption agencies to have regard, as far as practicable, to the wishes of the child's parents as to the child's religious upbringing.

"Guardian" has the same meaning as in **C.A. 1989.** An unmarried father is not a "parent" unless he has been given parental responsibility.

A mother's agreement is ineffective if given within six weeks of the child's birth.

Dispensing with parental agreement

Section 52 of the **A.C.A. 2002** gives the court power to dispense with consent on only two grounds:

(a) that the parent cannot be found or is incapable of giving consent; or

(b) that the welfare of the child requires it.

Freeing for adoption and placement orders

A freeing order vests parental responsibility in the adoption agency until an adoption order is made and terminates any order made under the **Children Act 1989**. On the face of it, a freeing order assists both agencies and adopters in removing the uncertainties from the process. In practice it has been little used, principally because of delays in the judicial process in making the freeing order.

Consequently, the **A.C.A. 2002** abolished freeing orders.

If Local Authorities wish to place a child in their care for adoption, they must apply for a placement order (s.22(1)(2)). Unless a care order has been made, the significant harm test must be satisfied and parental consent given or dispensed with. But the order can be challenged by the child's family and the welfare criteria are applied.

Revision Checklist

By now you should know and understand:

- **the meaning of Adoption and the persons who may be adopted and those who can adopt**

- **the legal process for adoption**

- **the alternative orders available to the Court**

QUESTION AND ANSWER

The Question

Lily, aged 6, has been living with her grandmother Alice for 2 years. Alice is her foster carer, placed by the Local Authority because her mother Jane has alcohol and other addiction problems. Recently, Jane has been making abusive and threatening phone calls and Alice seeks your advice as to what steps she may take to protect her position with Lily.

Suggested Answer

Alice has two options: to apply for adoption or for a Special Guardian Order.

If she were to apply for adoption, she would become Lily's legal mother and end Jane's relationship with Lily. However, Jane would have to consent to the order unless the court would dispense with that requirement on the grounds of the child's welfare.

In the alternative, she could be made the child's guardian which would give her parental responsibility but allow Jane to remain Lily's parent. In the end, the decision will be at the court's discretion, as always applying the welfare principle which is the paramount consideration.

HANDY HINTS AND USEFUL WEBSITES

Having studied the previous chapters, you may wish to test your knowledge and understanding by attempting the examination checklist of questions below. If you need to jog your memory, refer back to the relevant parts of the chapter. T his should help your revision.

It may also be helpful, when revising, to review once more the sample questions and answers given at the end of each chapter.

In addition to committing the law to memory, thinking about how to answer questions on a particular topic is important. If the examiner sets a problem question, try to address the problems raised rather than just writing everything you know about the topic. In an unseen examination, you will not know in advance what the questions and/or topics will be, but you will get some guidance from the tutorial and seminar questions your tutors will have set during your course of study.

EXAMINATION REVISION CHECKLIST

CHAPTER 1

1) The existing ground for divorce in the **M.C.A.** 1973 is irretrievable breakdown of the marriage as evidenced by one of the five facts.

2) Remember that adultery has to be accompanied with intolerable to live with, that behaviour is that which the petitioner finds unreasonable and two years' desertion requires intention. Living apart for two years requires consent and the defence of grave hardship only applies to the five years living apart.

CHAPTER 2

3) On breakdown of marriage, note the range of orders available to the court under the **M.C.A.**: lump sums, periodical payments, secured or unsecured, property adjustment orders or any combination thereof. Be aware of the court's greater involvement in ancillary relief proceedings.

4) The court has a discretion that it exercises with the help of the matters to be taken into account under s.25 of the **M.C.A.**:

(a)   income, earning capacity, property and other financial resources;
(b)   financial needs and obligations;
(c)   standard of living before breakdown;
(d)   age and duration of marriage;
(e)   disabilities;
(f)   contributions to the welfare of the family;
(g)   conduct if "inequitable to disregard it"; and
(h)   value of any benefit which they lose the chance of acquiring by reason of the dissolution.

Remember that the HL in *Piglowska* said that there is no ranking order.

5)   Children are a first consideration but note *Suter v Suter*.

6)   *White v White* is a landmark decision: note well its approaches. Fairness is the objective: equality is the "yardstick". No discrimination between the wage earner and the "homemaker" and disapproval of the former decisions in big money cases that only reasonable needs had to be considered.

7)   You should also be aware of the *McFarlane and Miller* decisions, expanding on fairness, introducing the compensation element and dealing with "non-matrimonial assets".

8)   Can the court make the parties self-sufficient to encourage a "clean break"?

9)   Under (h) above, there are now powers to earmark pensions or to split them. Be sure you know the difference between the two.

CHAPTER 3

10)   If the parties are not divorcing (or are unmarried), what are the rules to establish common ownership of their home? Is there evidence of a common intention? Has there been detrimental reliance and has the claimant made a contribution? Note the more generous approach of the CA in *Midland Bank v Cooke* and *Stack v Dowden* compared to the HL in *Pettitt, Gissing and Rosset*.

CHAPTER 4

11)   Note the demise of the Child Support Agency, the new Commissions powers to enforce agreements for maintenance and the residual powers in the **M.C.A.** and s.15 of the **Children Act**.

CHAPTER 5

12) When it comes to protection from violence, Pt IV of the **Family Law Act 1996** is in force. Learn who are "associated persons" for the purpose of proceedings.

13) What is an occupation order? What matters are taken into account before an order is made? Can you deal with the "balance of harm test"?

14) Be sure that you understand that orders have different duration depending on the relationship between the parties.

15) What is molestation and who can apply for a non-molestation order? How does it differ from harassment under the **Protection from Harassment Act 1997**?

CHAPTER 6

16) Who are the parents of a child born by natural means and what presumptions can be applied? Who are parents of children born by "human assisted reproduction"?

17) What is the law in relation to surrogacy agreements? How can commissioning parents become legal parents of the surrogate child?

18) Under the **Children Act 1989,** note that the welfare of the child is the paramount consideration in all contested proceedings under the Act. Be aware of the matters contained in the welfare checklist.

19) The emphasis of the **Children Act** is parental responsibility. Although there is no definition, you should be able to list some of the more important issues that the common law has identified.

20) Who has parental responsibility as of right? How can it be acquired?

CHAPTER 7

21) You should be able to explain the range and scope of s.8 orders and who can apply for them.

CHAPTER 8

22) In public law, what is the responsibility of local authorities for children in need in their area?

23) What is the "threshold criteria" and what is its significance in care proceedings?

24) What orders are available to local authorities to assist them in establishing whether or not a child is in need when parents will not co-operate?

25) If the threshold criteria are met, what orders can be made and what is the effect of them?

26) Is the court bound to make the orders sought in public law cases?

27) What do you understand by "wardship"? Does it still have a role in children's proceedings?

CHAPTER 9

28) Be aware of the effects of adoption, who can be adopted and who can adopt.

29) What do you understand by Special Guardians? What are their rights and responsibilities?

USEFUL WEBSITES

http://www.education.gov.uk/—Department for Education

http://www.parliament.uk/business/publications/hansard/lords/—House of Lords debates

http://lawcommission.justice.gov.uk/index.htm—Law Commission website

http://www.justice.gov.uk—Ministry of Justice

http://www.justice.gov.uk/about/hmcts/—Her Majesty's Court Service

http://iclr.co.uk/—Incorporated Council of Law Reporting

http://www.legislation.gov.uk/—Statute Law Database

http://www.thefma.co.uk/—Family Mediators Association

http://www.familylawweek.co.uk/site.aspx?i=ho0—Although aimed at practitioners, has weekly updates on recent cases and statutes

Index

This index has been prepared using Sweet and Maxwell's Legal Taxonomy. Main index entries conform to keywords provided by the Legal Taxonomy except where references to specific documents or non-standard terms (denoted by quotation marks) have been included. These keywords provide a means of identifying similar concepts in other Sweet and Maxwell publications and on-line services to which keywords from the Legal Taxonomy have been applied. Readers may find some differences between terms used in the text and those which appear in the index.

121